CREATIVITY

FOR

CRITICAL

THINKERS

CREATIVITY

FOR

CRITICAL

THINKERS

Anthony Weston

New York   Oxford
OXFORD UNIVERSITY PRESS
2007

Oxford University Press, Inc., publishes works that further Oxford
University's objective of excellence in research, scholarship, and education.

Oxford   New York
Auckland   Cape Town   Dar es Salaam   Hong Kong   Karachi
Kuala Lumpur   Madrid   Melbourne   Mexico City   Nairobi
New Delhi   Shanghai   Taipei   Toronto

With offices in
Argentina   Austria   Brazil   Chile   Czech Republic   France   Greece
Guatemala   Hungary   Italy   Japan   Poland   Portugal   Singapore
South Korea   Switzerland   Thailand   Turkey   Ukraine   Vietnam

Published by Oxford University Press, Inc.
198 Madison Avenue, New York, New York 10016
http://www.oup.com

Library of Congress Cataloging-in-Publication Data

Weston, Anthony, 1954–
    Creativity for critical thinkers / by Anthony Weston.
      p. cm.
    Includes bibliographical references.
    ISBN-13: 978-0-19-530621-7 (pbk. : alk. paper)
    ISBN 0-19-530621-X (pbk. : alk. paper)
      1. Creative ability.   2. Critical thinking.   I. Title.

BF408.W48 2006
153.3'5—dc22   2005057703

9 8 7 6 5 4 3 2 1

Printed in the United States of America
on acid-free paper

CONTENTS

PREFACE

Creativity is *the art of expanding possibility*. It is the art of finding unexpected space in problems that seem totally stuck to everyone else. It is the ability to think "out of the box" while the rest of us barely realize that we are *in* a box. Despite what we're often told, creativity in this sense is a readily learnable skill. This book aims to teach it—briefly and practically.

Specifically, this books aims to teach creativity for *critical thinkers*. The term "critical thinking" points toward certain skills now widely taught, such as a keen eye for arguments, the ability to look past vivid but possibly misleading examples and analogies, and fair-mindedness when our own favorite beliefs are under the knife. All vital skills, and skills I treasure and teach myself. Too often, though, especially in the hands of those just coming to learn it, "critical thinking" is reduced to mere *criticism*—a mostly negative and judgmental attitude that embraces new ideas only in the most guarded way, if at all, and is certainly not equipped to generate new ideas itself.

This book offers a more expansive view. To be able to see the world in the light of possibility is a vital thinking skill as well. Even the most specific argument or explanation, after all, must be evaluated partly against the background of what else is possible or how else the same events or correlations can be explained. By showing us the world, or some part of the world, as it *could* be, creativity gives us a whole new view of the world as it *is*.

Besides, the aim of criticism is to be constructive in the end: to make a difference. Here, especially, it is the creative part—the capacity to invent three or ten new ideas, to get "stuck" problems *un*stuck—that is the biggest contribution. Critical thinking can show us the need for new ideas, and can filter or elaborate them, but without creativity it only walks on one leg.

Oh, but "I'm not creative," we say. As if creativity were a genetic trait, like eye color or body type, beyond anyone's ability to change.

This book, I hope, will persuade you otherwise. The fact is that you can easily become more creative, using a few methods you know and trust. I don't promise that you will turn into a Picasso or an Einstein, but almost all of us can do far better than we do now, partly because so few of us are trained in creative thinking at all. Even a few methods can go a very long way.

General readers will find this book useful, I hope, as an engaging quick introduction to creative thinking. Teachers will wish to use it, I hope, in classrooms and workshops, and in particular might use it as a supplementary book for a university or high school class in critical thinking. Check out the "Notes and Sources" section at the end of the book for advice about how to use this book in such a class. It won't carry the whole class by itself, of course—for the more familiar argument-analysis and logical skills you will have to look elsewhere—but it *will* add an indispensable and sometimes even electrifying element. Don't slight the extensive exercises at the end of each chapter, which often contain new material as well.

This book has a sister, *Creative Problem-Solving in Ethics*, also published by Oxford University Press, offering similar creative tools but focused on creativity in practical ethics. Check it out if you get to the end of this book and find that you want more examples and applications and a few new creative tools as well. Creativity is as vital in ethics as anywhere else—possibly even more vital, since it usually gets even less play in ethics than in other realms of life. *Creativity for Critical Thinkers* mostly stays out of ethics only because I have offered a full-length treatment of creativity in ethics in a separate book.

Conversations with colleagues, students, and classes far too numerous to list have shown me again and again how intriguing and liberating most people find the whole topic of creativity. A sense of possibility and hope opens up, even when facing the stickiest or most troublesome problems. So I thank the many teachers who have invited me to speak on these points and/or who have reported to me how helpful these tools have proved to their students. For close reading and useful suggestions, I am grateful to my departmental colleagues at Elon University, especially Ann Cahill and Joe Cole. At Oxford University Press, my hat is off to my intrepid editor Robert B. Miller and Oxford's reviewers for this project: Paul Durbin, Cara Finnegan, Jeffrey Fry, and Dave Yount.

I also want to thank my own students over recent years, who have provoked many themes and changes and are starting to contact me with the big ideas that they have been working on, since the class, by themselves. And I welcome YOU, now, as you start down the same path. I wish you the best of luck, and heartily welcome all readers' comments, criticisms, and suggestions.

Anthony Weston
Durham, NC
weston@elon.edu

CREATIVITY

FOR

CRITICAL

THINKERS

1

CREATIVITY'S PROMISE

AT THE BUS STOP

A dark and stormy night. You are driving along in your sporty little two-seater. You come to a bus stop. Three people are waiting for the bus. One is a stranger who at that very moment keels over with a heart attack. Next is an old friend who once saved your life. The last, believe it or not, is the man or woman of your dreams. Who do you pick up?

This little brain-teaser apparently was used on a real job application as a test of creativity. At first glance there is no good answer. Or maybe too many. The stranger clearly needs to get to a hospital as quickly as possible. Your old friend could also use a ride, and you certainly owe her. But then there is the man or woman of your dreams, who otherwise you may never see again. And you have only one seat in your car . . .

So what do you think? How creative are you? Think about it for a moment before reading on. What would you do?

Legend has it that the winning job candidate (out of 200) hesitated not at all before giving his answer: "I would give the car keys to my old friend and ask her to take the stranger to the hospital, and then I would stay behind and wait for the bus with the woman of my dreams."

Now think about this answer. If you're like most people, you approached the problem by mentally reviewing your options. And the way your mind shaped this mental review was to imagine taking each of the three people in your car in turn. "I could take the stranger, but then. . . ." "I could take the man or woman of my dreams, but then. . . ." What most people do *not* do is ask themselves if there are any options *besides* taking one of the three people in your car with you as the driver. Ask this question, though, and you are immediately "out of the box"—and then coming up with a great answer is easy.

So one moral of this story is that "thinking out of the box" is not so hard to learn. After all, "What about *other* options?" is not exactly a hard question to learn to ask.

There is another moral as well. *Even situations that seem totally "stuck" have unsuspected possibilities.*

People who pride themselves on being "practical"—maybe you yourself just a moment ago—might look at this situation and declare, "Well, you just have to decide! Obviously there are three and only three possibilities. Just decide and get on with it!" But you know now that this is bad advice. "*Obviously* there are three and only three possibilities"? As no less an expert than Sherlock Holmes once said, what's obvious isn't always true. There *are* other possibilities. What is really practical is to start looking for them.

WHAT IS CREATIVITY?

Creativity is *the ability to cast a situation or challenge or problem in a new light and thereby open up possibilities in it that were not evident before.*

Creative people are *critical*: they don't stop with the "given" and the (supposedly) "obvious." They are *imaginative*: they make a habit of thinking in more open and supple ways, keeping their minds two steps ahead of things as they are. They are *inventive*: they consciously seek to devise new things and new ways of thinking.

And creative people are *disciplined* and *persistent*. Creativity can require a certain kind of playfulness—as we shall soon see—but it does not mean just letting go. Creativity takes *work*. Thomas Edison famously said that genius is 1% inspiration and 99% perspiration. Maybe he overstated a little—I'd say it's 20% inspiration and 80% perspiration—but that's still a lot of sweat.

A ROCKY START

Now a professional scenario. You're an architect supervising the excavation for a new house. The minute the backhoe starts digging, it hits an enormous rock. Immovable, like a wall. What do you do?

Well, there are ways to move even the immovable. A week or two later, maybe, after a nice big investment in bulldozers or explosives, you can have your hole—maybe now so nice and big that you have to spend more time partly filling it back in with fragments of the rock you've just laboriously blown to bits.

Well, that's life, right? Or is it? Now that you have a little encouragement to look for creative solutions, you might not jump so fast with the dynamite. Didn't you learn a little creativity back in architecture school?

One useful question is, "Are there better ways to get rid of the rock?" Maybe it has some cracks you could use to break it into pieces. Maybe you could rig up your backhoe with pulleys and winch it out. Or maybe—getting a *little* more creative—you could dig an even deeper hole and roll it in.

There's a little space in this. Basically, though, it's more of the same, like asking which of the three people at the bus stop you should take into your car. Try instead for a better question.

"How do we move the rock?" we've been asking. But now suppose we ask, "What if we did not move the rock?" Are there other possible ways to get around this problem?

New possibilities emerge the minute we ask this new question. One is, "Why not move the *house*—build it away from the rock? Must the house be right there?" Six feet to the right or the left, maybe, a little adjustment in your plans, and there would be no problem.

Notice again that this is a different kind of question from the original. Maybe dynamite would be the best way to get rid of the rock—but maybe getting rid of the rock is not the best way to get rid of the *problem*. We need a little more mental flexibility, in place of the straight-ahead mentality that simply perceives a problem, defines it in one way, and charges ahead (and calls itself "practical"!). Problem-solving expert Edward de Bono—we'll hear more from him presently—instead advocates what he calls "lateral thinking." When you begin to imagine moving the whole house, you have stepped back from the immediate situation and begun to explore ways to sidestep the problem entirely.

Is there another step you might take with this problem too? Suppose you ask whether this rock is really a problem at all. Could there be a way to use this unexpected obstacle to advantage?

At first, this may seem totally improbable, even senseless. "How could the rock not be a problem? Here is where I meant to put the house—there is a rock! House or rock, something's got to give!"

Does it? Really?

An immovable rock, like a wall, eh? Suppose it *were* a wall? How about building the house around the rock? A really creative architect might redesign the house itself, maybe making a fireplace in the "natural" rock wall. . . . So now the house might be far more dramatic and intriguing, not to mention less expensive, than it would have been otherwise. The rock is put to use, and what a fine use it might be! Neither house nor rock moves, no dynamite is required, the homeowner ends up with a truly unique house, for less money . . . where's the problem?

THE FIRST STEP TOWARD CREATIVITY IS TO CHANGE OUR VERY IDEA OF A "PROBLEM"

Typically, today, the term "problem" has negative overtones. Problems are to be regretted, avoided, stuffed back in their box as quickly as possible. The temptation is to find the first half-decent answer and stop. Who wants to "have problems"?

We should. Seriously—we should. We need to think of problems as occasions for ongoing thinking, as invitations to be imaginative. From this point of view we should *welcome* problems, even seek them out. Problems are our opportunities to change the world. Nothing less than that.

Notice that in this way we are invited to critically rethink our very problems themselves. For the architect, for example, real creativity begins not by finding better ways to move the rock, but at the next step: thinking of moving the *house*. You are no longer addressing the "given" problem at all. Using the rock for a wall of the house, meanwhile, is not a solution of anything like the original problem. You can transform the given problem not merely into another problem—useful as that often might be—but into a genuine opportunity instead.

Think of our usual dislike of problems as a kind of *push*. We have a difficulty that makes us uncomfortable and therefore motivates us, however reluctantly and without much confidence, to try to remove the discomfort. Any old Band-Aid will probably do. Let's just get it over with.

Recognize the space for creative transformation, however, and motivation works from the other direction. Now we are *pulled* toward something better. Band-Aids are no longer enough. We're not interested in just papering over the problem and going back to sleep. We must speak of *inspiration* here—certainly of persistence, confidence, energy. Also, even, of fun (and if you don't believe that, just wait a chapter or two).

Moreover, as we shall soon see, all of this is true even of "problems" on the largest scale. There are creative opportunities in everything from the smallest everyday annoyance to the business world and the largest of social issues. You can even make a well-paid career out of creatively tackling them. Unexpected and even quite wonderful possibilities are there for the finding. But, of course, we need to *look* for them!

FOR PRACTICE ❖

1. Here are some questions to think about.

- What are your own associations with the word "problem"? Welcome, unwelcome? Why?

- Do specific kinds of problems come to mind? How have you dealt with them in the past? Are there ways you'd like to improve? Are there places in your life right now where you feel that you need some creativity? Could other people use some creativity too: political leaders, say, or teachers, taxi drivers, orthodontists, burglars . . . ?

- Do you know people whose creativity is inspiring to you? Talk to them: find out how they do it.
- What do you hope to gain from this book?

2. In most of this book, we will take on a variety of practical problems—personal, social, scientific, philosophical—and try to rethink them creatively. By way of warming up, though, I invite you to try a few wilder questions, mostly to get a sense of just how wide a space creative thinking might open up. Play with these; don't get tangled up in them; just exercise your imagination, stretch your mental muscles a little.

- Have all possible political systems already been invented? Really? Can you imagine something truly new? How about at least a few major improvements to our system as it currently exists?
- Have all possible forms of art been invented? It's not likely: just think of the emergence recently of digital art, computer music, whale song, highly developed graffiti styles, "re-art" (art using wholly recycled materials), etc. What else is possible? Invent a few new forms of art yourself. (Weather art? Something involving roads? Smells?)
- How do you think we might solve the environmental crisis? You know the usual answer: by trying to cut way back on pollution and waste, hard as that may be, and hoping to muddle through. What else could you imagine?
- What if time travel were possible? What totally new possibilities might arise? An empirical resolution to the evolution-versus-creation debate? Wars between alternative futures, fought in the present, as in the *Terminator* films? Vacations with the dinosaurs? Recently I found a website that for the modest fee of $10 promises to invest some of it for a few hundred years, when even a single dollar at compound interest becomes several billion, and then use (a little of) the money to come back and whisk you off to a well-endowed and long-lived future (maybe immediately upon sending in your $10—what are you waiting for?). Clever, huh? And suppose this kind of thing were just the beginning?

- If you could use genetic engineering to totally remake human beings, how would you do it? Don't stop with external stylistic improvements, like adding gills so we can breathe under water (for some reason a perennial favorite). How about creating people without the capacity, say, for certain kinds of violence or fanaticism? Making us photosynthetic (like plants, absorbing energy directly from the sun) so we wouldn't need to eat for energy? What else can you think of?

- How many different ways can you imagine that the universe might have come into being? Usually we're invited to consider only two options: that it was intentionally created all at once, in all its intricacy and scope, by a Cosmic Architect; or that it exploded into beginning (the "Big Bang") and evolved from there. What *else* do you think might be possible? We do know that there are other ways that things come into being: through plant or animal (cellular) reproduction, for example. Could the universe have originated like that? Or maybe in some other way unique to universes? Such as?

2

GETTING STARTED

THE FORCE OF HABIT

Not long ago, it was almost impossible to get morphine—one
of the most powerful of painkillers—even if you were dying in
severe pain. Families and doctors feared that morphine was
addictive. Morphine is an opiate and was heavily used for the
wounded during the Civil War and again during World War I,
when it did create serious problems—though many sources
now report that, if properly used, it need not be addictive.

In any case, though, whether morphine is addictive or not,
it hardly matters when people are already on their deathbeds.
Yet somehow this little detail never quite registered. So for a
whole generation people died in unnecessary pain because—
well, why?

The answer isn't hard to see. It is *habit*. Reacting to the addiction caused by the overuse of morphine in the past, doctors acquired a habit of avoidance that became instinctual. It also didn't help, I'm sure, that morphine is closely associated with other opiates—heroin, for one—so that the moral connotation of "drug" also stuck in people's minds.

So that's where we were: stuck. Strange as it now seems, it was not possible to break the old habits and associations even when (you would think) they clearly did not apply. For a long time, people literally could not *see* the absurdity of denying morphine to dying people. Habits became blinders. Lately we see more clearly on this issue—morphine is accepted, though still with reservations—but, of course, it makes you wonder what other, similar absurdities are still staring us in the face.

Psychologists have a word to describe these mental blinders, these habits and assumptions and fixed ways of seeing: "set." "Set" isn't always a bad thing. We can't figure everything out from the beginning every time we need to do something—we'd never do anything. Most of the time we have to rely on our habits to get us through, adding in a little thinking only when necessary. Lucky for us.

Unluckily for us, though, "set" also blocks *new* ways of seeing. It blocks flexibility and creativity. Sometimes the ruts of habit can be so deep that we can't see over the top of them, so to speak, which means we can't even see that we're in them. And then we're really stuck.

THE NEED FOR A METHOD

The moral of the story is that we need *methods* to help us break "set," or "think outside the box." It's not enough for someone just to say "Be creative!" or "Break out of your habits!" Without any further help, we'll still just take another couple of trips around the same old circles and end up in pretty much the same place. I've seen too many people do just that, sitting with furrowed brows, tensing the mental muscles—the very image of Someone Thinking Really Hard— and getting nowhere.

To break out, we need to loosen up, try something new. Maybe even something peculiar, embarrassing, or improbable. It may feel forced, but that's just the point: you're trying to entice yourself out beyond your own habits, out of the mental "box" which confines you, beyond the familiar world that is so comforting but can also be so constraining. "Boxes" like these can be very strong. We need some equally forceful ways to shake things up a bit, to see the world in a broader way.

So expect some unusual and maybe even awkward methods. You may be tempted not to take them seriously or use them only half-heartedly. Don't! They may seem silly, awkward, even embarrassing (anyway to do in public); but *this is just what they need to be.* The whole point is to get out beyond your safety zone, the familiar round that is also where you are "stuck." Play along, trust the process ... take the leap.

INVITING EXOTIC ASSOCIATIONS

This chapter introduces a first method—just one—for "thinking out of the box." By looking at a single method, we can explore it in enough detail that you get a good sense of how to use it and what it can do. You may find it surprising, though it is in fact one of the most widely recommended methods by creativity experts. You may also, I suspect, find it surprisingly effective.

The method is this. Start with any random "prompt" at all, then ask what new ideas or associations it provokes when put together with your problem or question. The prompt itself can come from anywhere—literally *anywhere:* walking down the street, chance words in a conversation, a film, a dictionary, a textbook, a mystery, a dream, a magazine. If you are using words, usually it is best to have a source with a varied and rich vocabulary—find a good classic writer, maybe—but in a pinch you can even take words from billboards along the freeway or by turning on the car radio for two seconds, as I sometimes do if I am using this method while driving. When I'm writing, sometimes even an accidental misspelling suggests a new idea or a more vivid turn of phrase.

This method I call "inviting exotic associations." The point is: find as truly random a source of associations as you can. Now you really have a "prompt"—a new, unfiltered stimulus to your thinking—from outside your rut. Right away something fresh. And easy!

I have to tell you, though, that in my experience, despite the lead-up I just gave, most people's first reaction to this method is still, "That's silly! *Exotic* associations? With *random* prompts?" So I have to say it again: a little silliness may be just what we need. Randomness—generating possible prompts without filters—is exactly what it may take to break out of the rut that we happen to be in (but can't quite see).

Anyway, patience. . . . At least give the method a chance to show what it can do, eh?

A FIRST EXAMPLE

You've seen exercises in brain-teaser books asking you to think of some everyday functional object like a brick or a cheap ballpoint pen and imagine what else could be done with it. The challenge is to invent not just one or two new uses but maybe ten or twenty-five. Stretch your mind, in short—like physical exercise.

So let us try it with, say, *a burned-out light bulb*.

Pretty unpromising, right? On the face of it, there's nothing to do with a burned-out light bulb at all. Just toss it. But now let's try to get creative.

With no method at all you might come up with a few new uses. Paint the bulb and use it for a Christmas tree ornament, maybe. Extending the same idea, flashlight bulbs might make nice earrings. But probably those are about all the ideas that readily come to mind. We have two, and we need a lot more.

Try the exotic-association method. A quick and easy way would be to try using random words. As it happens, amidst the debris on my desk right now I have Bill Bryson's book *In a Sunburned Country*, a rollicking Australian travelogue—certainly a random source in this context. Opening it without looking, I just drop my finger onto the page and there is a word: "cork-like."

That's certainly random! (As it happens, Bryson is writing about how his airplane seemed to pop out of the clouds one day.) Again, it will seem silly. But wait—give it a second—let's think. Could there be possibilities even in this (literally) out-of-the-blue prompt?

Hmm ... could a burned-out light bulb be made into some kind of bottle stopper (that is, like a cork)? Or what if it *had* a stopper—that is, if it itself were made into some sort of container? Free-associating, this reminds me of how in some specialty stores you see old wine bottles that have been cut in half to make a mug (the bottom) and a wine glass (the top, turned upside down and with a base). So what about light bulbs? Of course, the glass is a lot thinner, but some glasses are made that way—classy. So, how about making them into champagne glasses? Their fragility is now part of their appeal.

Notice already: this is a truly new idea, definitely "out of the box" compared to how I was thinking just a minute ago. Nor did I just mechanically "apply" my random word (that is, champagne glasses aren't cork-like and they don't themselves have corks). No, the prompt did just what it was supposed to do: *start* me along a new path. A *new* path. One free association opened up the field for others.

Maybe there's something to this exotic-association method after all?

Bryson, word 2: "battlefield." Hmm ... what about smashing the bulb and using the base, with its jagged edges remaining, as a weapon? Since there are light bulbs nearly everywhere, you can almost always get yourself a weapon in a pinch.

Word 3: "likeable." Hmm ... maybe paint the bulb red and send it to someone as a valentine? Love is fragile ...

Word 4: "more." Plain vanilla, this time—but let's not prejudge it. OK, "more" what? Bulbs? Or maybe more use out of each bulb? Aha! Maybe we could figure out how to make a recyclable bulb, so that (ideally) we could replace just the filament and keep on using the glass casing. This idea comes partly from another association: the new style of auto headlight is now made like this, with the reflector and lens built into the car, rather than (as it used to be) a large bulb. All you change is the tiny tube-like bulb inside. How about replaceable filaments? Whole new business opportunities here.

We could go on, but you get the picture. Even in this very simplest of examples, just the briefest of random word associations gives us an entire set of new ideas. *After* we have generated some of these ideas, we can begin to see some of the "ruts" that confined our thinking originally. For instance, in ordinary imagination we think of bulbs as intact and fastened up or down—pretty much "normal" shape and positions. The random prompts pushed us into the *ab*normal. And a few pushes, it turns out, were all that we needed.

WEATHER REPORT BLUES

Now let us try the exotic-association method in a real case. Here is a problem that might confront you as a program manager for a local TV station. You're in charge of the news and weather shows as well as other programming, and you know the weather report, in particular, is lagging. You need some new ideas, and soon.

The problem is that weather reports are by nature unreliable, and the result can be frustrating. Everyone knows that weather forecasting is an inexact science, but most of us still have a few choice words for weather reports anyway, especially when the weather does not turn out as predicted. As manager, you need to keep the weather forecast in your program, but you know it is not boosting your show. You yourself find the weather report unappealing.

A natural strategy is to try to get more accurate weather information. But there are limits to this. It seems that the information you are getting is about as good as it gets—not good enough, yet, for the kind of appeal you'd like your show to have. You need to get creative in some other direction. But what?

Once again, let us generate some random prompts. This time, maybe, we'll use a dictionary. In fact, I'm going to go at random through the "P" section of my dictionary, free associating as I go. Remember, there are no strict rules—even the follow-on associations can (often should) be "random." Let us just try to unfold a few word-prompts and see where we get.

So: "Parcheesi." Right. Well, Parcheesi is a game. So, could a weather forecast be presented as a kind of game (that is, rather than a set of facts being conveyed)? Interesting. What kind of game? Maybe two weather reporters could compete with each other, each presenting a somewhat different forecast, and the station or the viewers keep score?

This leads to another idea: maybe the forecast could be presented as a kind of comedy. Make it humorous—even play on the uncertainty. Maybe if it rains when the forecaster said it wouldn't, the reporter should get drenched?

You see right away that there are some lovely possibilities here for generating new kinds of viewer interest. Either one of these could dramatically turn around your station's fortunes. And that's just the first word.

"Paris." Alright, what is the weather in Paris? Hmm . . . Would viewers be interested in that? Probably—just look at the popularity of the Weather Channel. So maybe the weather report should put more emphasis on what the weather *is*, here and elsewhere, rather than what it *will be*?

"Planetary." Maybe your station could do more reporting on the movements of the planets (and moon, stars, comets, eclipses, etc.)—astronomical events that, unlike the weather, actually *are* predictable and have their own beauty and appeal.

"President." How about setting up the weather report as a debate (like the presidential debates) between competing weather forecasters? This would create an engaging and unusual format and is ready-made for some humor as well as a little teaching.

"Principal" also suggests a kind of teaching, making weather reports a learning experience (why is the weather so complex? what are some of the factors now in play?), rather than simply predictions. After all, once again, aren't there opportunities precisely in the weather's uncertainty? Couldn't we approach it in a spirit of adventure and curiosity, rather than just impatience? Sure, weather reports are unreliable, but why couldn't this—precisely this—make the whole business *interesting*?

"Prize" suggests games and competitions. How about betting, too? Maybe viewers should be allowed to call in or place online bets on the accuracy of the reports, which the station could pay off with on-the-air attention or some other benefit that also promotes the station. Or maybe the station, when wrong, has to give away free rain gear (of course, with the station's logo).

Many more ideas are possible. But let us take a few steps back from the by-now-pretty-engaging process of devising them and just look at how much the problem seems to have changed. At the start it looked stuck—forecasting is just unreliable, and that's the way things are. Now it looks wide open. All sorts of creative formats are possible, even if the weather reports remain as unreliable as can be. Some of your new ideas even make a *virtue* of the weather reports' unreliability. I think you are going to do very well as this station's manager.

And now, most importantly, you know how to begin to generate some new ideas. It's not a matter of trying to force yourself to be more creative as if it were bench-pressing more weight. It's not a matter of more weight at all. The invitation is to a kind of playfulness instead: to get *lighter*. Thinking in *new* ways, seeking the unexpected and even random stimulus, feels almost weightless. And why *shouldn't* creativity be fun?

ENOUGH FOR NOW—ALMOST

We're still just starting, getting a feel for thinking in a new way. For now, let me add just a few quick guidelines and reminders for using free association as a creative method.

First, don't prejudge your prompts. That is, don't decide that a random image or word won't suggest any useful associations until you actually give it a try. Maybe give yourself a certain minimum time—say, three minutes (and use a timer: three minutes may be longer than you think)—to see what you can do with it. That is, *whatever* random prompt you come up with, give it *at least* three minutes of good free-associating time. Filtering out prompts in advance, or only half-trying with what you think is an unpromising prompt, may leave you stuck in the very rut you're trying to get out of. The prompts that seem least promising may even be your best ones, because they can lead you farthest "out of the box"—but, of course, you have to be willing to follow.

Second, and for the same reason, welcome unfamiliar or ridiculous or even (yes) taboo associations. They too can be suggestive—they may help you around problems that you simply can't solve head-on. Again, no prefiltering. There's plenty of time to do that later: the trick is usually in generating a lot of good material *to* edit.

Case in point: the pioneering German chemist August Kekulé's solution to the problem of the benzene molecule, which simply wouldn't fit the chain model of molecular structure that Kekulé had developed and that worked beautifully for other molecules. Kekulé struggled with this problem for seven years. One day he fell asleep in front of a fire and dreamt of serpents biting their tails. When he awoke, he realized that the benzene molecule might not be a long chain shape but instead a *ring*—and the vexing problem was solved. If he'd awakened annoyed, though, and said to himself "Let me get this nonsense about tail-biting serpents out of my head and get back to my problem!" he'd never have solved it.

Third, keep at it. Studies show that brainstormers tend to come up with the best ideas if they're simply asked to come up with the *most* ideas. If instead they're directly asked to come up with the best idea they can, they stop to fine-tune the first fairly decent idea they have. Don't stop too soon. The fourth idea, or the fourteenth idea, or maybe even the fortieth idea, may be the true act of genius.

Finally, don't *ever, ever, ever* say "I'm just not creative" in place of trying to do some creative thinking. Creativity is not a question of genes. It's right here in this book, and you have the book in front of you. Use it!

FOR PRACTICE ◈

1. Practice the exotic-association method by imagining new uses for all sorts of everyday objects, even the most boring, such as dirty socks or ballpoint pens or cement blocks or discarded Styrofoam packaging or cat litter, etc.

Assign yourself ten quick new ideas, then fifteen, then twenty. Invite your friends to play, figure out prizes for the coolest new ideas, figure out how to market the best of them.

Go on to use the random-word method specifically to create new names for school or professional sports teams. Right now there are, at best, only two or three types of names: predatory animals (Hawks, Tigers, etc.), maybe; warlike attitudes (Avengers, Spartans, etc.); a few sport-specific names (United in soccer); and that's about it. What else is possible? Musical terms? Food (Jambalaya? Fricassee? Cayenne Peppers?)? Landscapes? Cool colors? Made-up words?

How about names of restaurants? Names of stores?

Try the same approach to creative writing—either for whole story lines or for fresh words (say, in writing poetry).

2. Use the exotic-association method to tackle some small but troublesome daily problems right around us (we'll come to the big problems soon enough). Continue to allow yourself to get a little wild. Come up with some new possibilities; in fact, challenge yourself to triple or, say, quintuple the number of options usually considered. (And keep your notes—you'll need them again.)

- Bored? Think of new ideas or business opportunities to deal with boredom. A boredom hotline (call up and hear wild jokes, creative suggestions, etc.)? A new game: pretend you are someone else, or actually switch roles with them? Do a play with some neighborhood children (in fact, do *anything* with young children)? Make a virtue of boredom (slogan: "Is Your Life Too Exciting?")? Ok, how?

- What about the lack of inexpensive travel options? Can you imagine some totally different ways to travel? Or totally different ways to use the familiar means of travel? In Europe and Australia, there are cheap youth hostels even in the smallest towns. What would it take to do that in the United States? What might we do that might be even better?

- How about *waste* problems: litter, lights left on all the time, tons of discarded newspaper, etc.?

- Americans currently watch 250 billion hours of TV a year. The average elementary-school child watches four hours a day. (And you?) Supposing that you agree that this is a bit much, what are some creative ways of addressing the problem?

- Good child care is hard to find and even harder to afford for many families with young children. How might we approach this problem?

- How about your classes and your school in general? (I'll leave the list of problems to you.) What changes could you yourself actually make *right now* that might make a major difference?

- Driving along, you turn on the public radio station and groan "Not another fund drive!" But don't switch stations: use your exotic-association method to generate some alternatives to on-the-air fundraising for public radio. Call the station with your best ideas—they can be your contribution.

- Speaking of driving, what about all those uncivil drivers? Red-light runners, tailgaters, speeders? Traffic jams? Parking problems around school and home?

3

MULTIPLYING YOUR OPTIONS

We have looked at one creative method in detail—enough to get a sense of what "thinking out of the box" really feels like. Most importantly, you see what it takes: an exploratory attitude, a willingness to unsettle things a bit in search of new ideas and angles—and, first and foremost, *methods*.

Now we are ready to turn up the speed. This chapter introduces a variety of further creative methods, all in the same exploratory spirit.

GO PUBLIC

Other people have had experiences we've not had, ideas we've not yet thought of. They may see things in ways we cannot even imagine. Even someone's chance half-sentence may give you a perspective you didn't have before—if you ask, and if you are prepared to listen. So one great way to diversify and develop your ideas is simply to talk to other people. Right away you are likely to be getting other views and angles.

Try *anyone* else. Try people you've never talked to, even people who you might think could not possibly help you. Maybe *especially* such people. (Remember, filtering and pre-judging "prompts" is one good way to stay in a rut.) As a parent, I have had to learn again and again to ask my children, even when they could barely talk, for their thoughts and suggestions on family business—room decoration, vacation plans—for they always have completely unexpected (to me) angles on things, new ways of seeing.

A more organized way to "go public" is brainstorming—a group process for generating new ideas. Though we speak loosely of "brainstorming" for any attempt at creative thinking, the idea has a specific origin. Advertising executive Alex Osborne invented it (in 1939) as a deliberate process to facilitate creativity in groups. The key rule is to *defer criticism*. Welcome all new ideas without immediately focusing on the likely difficulties and problems. In this way, we give new ideas, still barely hatched, enough space to develop and link up with others, to pass around the room, to provoke other ideas in turn. *Then* you can start looking for problems.

Of course, it's tempting (and safer) to react right away to any new suggestion with doubts: it couldn't possibly work, people won't like it, on and on. Brainstorming asks us to do the opposite: to consider how some new idea *could* work, not why it probably won't. Even a crude and obviously unrealistic idea, passed around the room, may evolve into something much more realistic, and meanwhile it may spark other new ideas. Ideas piggyback on each other. But you have to help it happen.

Take the problem of littering around fast-food restaurants. Here's a little dialogue:

A: Maybe we'd be more likely to recycle if we realized that it takes far more energy to produce those wrappers and cans than we get out of the food or drink.

B: It does? Too bad we can't eat the wrappers and cans.

C: That's stupid.

D: Well, what if we *could* eat them?

B: Like an ice cream cone—it holds the ice cream while you eat, and then you eat the cone too. No mess.

A: Even if it got dirty, at least the dog might want it . . .

D: Dirt, huh? Maybe wrappers and cans could be made of some material that composts easily—you know, decomposes in a few weeks with water and sun.

B: You can shred up your newspapers now and put them right into the garden for mulch. Couldn't we have cans or wrappers like that?

At least two new and truly out-of-the-box ideas come out of this little exchange: the idea of edible wrappers and cans and the idea of wrappers and cans that readily decompose.

Notice again that it took time. The crucial step was to listen and to "spark": not to immediately criticize and judge other ideas, but to *work off* them to make a further association and take another step. (That's another key guideline in formal brainstorming work too: Osborne puts it as "Hitchhike on others' ideas.") We started out thinking just about how to get people to recycle a little more; we ended up thinking about, well, eating trash!

Poor C, though. He seems to think that his job is just to pass judgment on others' ideas, rather than add to them, develop or deepen them, or even offer an alternative. Reactions like C's

---

ASKING GOOD QUESTIONS

Imagine a meeting in which any new suggestion is met with comments like these:

- It will never work.
- We've never done it that way.
- The boss won't like it.
- If that's such a great idea, why hasn't it been done before?

You know what will happen: in short order, no one will make any more suggestions or try to explore those that are made. Defensiveness will become the name of the game, and only the most timid ideas will have a chance.

Creative thinkers ask *questions* instead—open-ended, exploratory, and, yes, supportive questions. Some constructive lead-ins are:

- I wonder if/why/whether . . .
- Maybe we could . . . or That would work if . . .
- In what ways might we . . .

Edward de Bono abbreviates the last lead-in as IWW. It's a handy little abbreviation to put before assertions in your mind's eye (or on paper). Rather than "People would never do this!" say instead "IWW (in what ways) might people start to do this?" Verbally it may seem a small thing, but conceptually it is a great leap. The first statement is a categorical rejection. The second is a question: it invites a joint exploration of possibilities.

---

could derail such a conversation. But notice the spirit in which the others take them here. They keep right on thinking in a more open-ended way. The ideas keep flowing. And in the long run, C may come around too.

By the way, both edible and decomposable wrappers are under development. Both ideas are "wild" but also, it turns out, *realistic*.

COMPARE AND CONTRAST

Even the wildest (to us) arrangements have probably been normal for some group of people somewhere and sometime, probably even now. Did they learn anything from this? Could we? The great variety of human lives at the very least offers an excellent source of new ideas, whether in the end we adopt (or adapt) them or not. Learning from others, in short, need not be limited to conversations or brainstorming. We have history and cross-cultural comparison to learn from as well.

Do you know that Australian college students can go to college first and pay later—when they have more money? That marijuana is legal in Amsterdam (and the result is not disaster)? That English toilets don't leak—whereas the flap system used in the United States wastes billions of gallons of water through leaks? That most traditional societies had matchmakers to help young people find the right mates, rather than trusting young people's judgment, which can easily be swayed and unrealistic?

Taxicabs and trucks in Singapore have little alarms and flashing lights that go on if the vehicle speeds. Everyone knows when you're speeding (and the cops don't need radar). Some of them are even made so that they don't go off until the driver goes down to the police office and pays a fine. Why not in the United States?

Many Mediterranean countries still practice *siesta,* a long period of rest and quiet in the middle of the day. Again, why not in the United States? The siesta lessens the crush of work, instead of pushing it all into a single eight-hour stretch, and it might even help reduce American energy consumption, since part of the point of the siesta is to take off work during the hottest part of the day.

One of my Hindu colleagues even defends arranged marriages, which she says fail no more than American marriages, almost half of which now end in divorce. There *must* be better ways, don't you think? (Matchmakers? What would be a modern/American equivalent? Probably some great business opportunities here.)

You see, anyway, how ideas begin to flow. We may even discover that problems that seem totally bogged down to us are not problems at all for other people or at other times. Abortion, for example, one of the United States' most divisive social conflicts over the past thirty years, is barely an issue in most other countries (for somewhat different and sometimes opposite reasons). Historically, it was not even much of an issue here—and when it was, conservatives originally *favored* relaxed abortion laws, while liberals had their doubts (check it out). This history does not automatically generate solutions, of course, but it does give us a sense of possibility. The problem is more open-ended than it looks. We're only "stuck" (only seem to be stuck) *right now*.

You may need to do some research. Look into the comparisons and contrasts. If legal marijuana is not a problem in Amsterdam, why not? (Don't assume that the only difference is a few laws—find out!) If abortion is not such an issue in Japan, why not? How do they manage? (It turns out they have certain rituals of acknowledgment and closure—so again: why not in the United States?)

EXAGGERATE!

Exotic association is one—but only one—way to deliberately create wild provocations for yourself. There are others. Again, the aim is not to immediately produce a usable idea but to open up "the box," to generate novel possibilities, to push yourself to look at familiar things in totally unexpected ways.

One excellent way is *exaggeration*. That is, take some feature of the problem and push it as far as it can go.

TAKING HINTS

You're beginning to see, I hope, that the raw materials for creativity are all around us all the time. Offhand remarks by other people, or even ourselves. A child's prattle. Odd facts about other places or times. Random words that come our way—even random misspellings while typing. Dreams, even jokes, both of which can combine images or ideas in unexpected and suggestive ways.

The challenge is to stay open to all of this. Usually, we dismiss or ignore it, even find it irritating. "Jokes, trivia, dreams—really!?" But again: if the task is to break "set," to get out of our ruts and think out of the box, then we should welcome just such provocations. *Of course* they are not going to look realistic or relevant at first. But suppose—just suppose—that you think of them as the world giving you hints, making suggestions, offering possibilities. Can you let yourself be provoked?

There are other kinds of "hint," too. Accidents, for example. Sticky pads were an unintended by-product of 3M's search for a really strong adhesive. They ended up with a really weak adhesive instead. Failure? Maybe—until someone thought to ask if weak adhesives might have some uses too.

Flaked cereal (Corn Flakes, etc.) was invented when someone at Kellogg's unintentionally left some cereal paste to dry too long. Penicillin was discovered because Alexander Fleming accidentally exposed some of his bacteria cultures. Most people would have just thrown out the samples without even looking at them. But Fleming looked, and carefully enough to notice some unusual bacterial die-off. The rest is history. "Sometimes you find what you are not looking for."

Take a familiar problem like speeding—people driving too fast. Usually our only response is more enforcement: more cops. Creative rethinking could start, maybe, by exaggerating *that*: that is, imagining cops everywhere. I guess then almost everyone would have to be a cop. Not too likely, but keep at it. Are there ways in which we could all act *like* cops? What if anyone could turn in a speeder? That would require, at the least, some sort of radar in every car. But this leads to yet another idea. Suppose lots of people had just the radar generators—the read-back part wouldn't be necessary. If you'd rather be surrounded by nice, law-abiding drivers than by speeders, just hit your radar button and speeders' radar detectors will start to spasm. That's not a half-bad idea (and actually, you can buy this kind of generator now).

Faster speeds produce bumpier rides. Suppose we exaggerate this feature of roads—what if rides get *really* bumpy at higher speeds? Crazy, right? Or maybe not. If roads were engineered so that unpleasant vibrations are set up in car frames when the speed limit is exceeded (say with a special kind of small speed bump—it's quite feasible), then roads could enforce their own speed limits. That's a really good idea!

And wouldn't it be nice if cars themselves reminded us of some of the dangers of speed? How to exaggerate here? How about recordings of car crashes coming over your car stereo if you hit the accelerator too hard? Big spikes in the middle of the steering wheel? OK, maybe not—but once again these wild and maybe even offensive ideas start us thinking. Surely there are more graphic ways to remind people, right in the car, just how dangerous speeding can be?

Another use of exaggeration is what de Bono calls the method of the "intermediate impossible." Imagine a *perfect* solution to your problem, he says, however unrealistic. Then work your way back to a realistic idea from there. Make your very first imaginative step a really big one. It's easier to tone it down later than to ramp up a timid little half-step idea into something bigger.

Case in point: we have all had the frustration of misplacing our car keys. Tackling the problem in an incremental and "realistic" way, we might tie our keys to our clothes or purse, maybe, or look for new ways to hide spare keys outside of the

THINKING AT THE SPEED OF LIGHT

Albert Einstein started his professional life as a clerk in the Swiss Patent Office, capping off an undistinguished school career (supposedly he even failed math). He did physics in his spare time and without equipment. What he did have was imagination. And his key insights were the result of radical exaggeration.

In particular, Einstein arrived at his General Theory of Relativity by imagining what it would be like to travel at the speed of light—or rather, more exactly, trying to figure out how the passage of time would be affected if one frame of reference were moving at or close to the speed of light relative to another.

This is not exactly realistic. The speed of light is immensely greater than the speed anyone has ever traveled or perhaps ever will travel. Einstein's was a pure "thought-experiment," but it allowed him to begin to see what we can't see when we are dealing with things in our normal world: that time passes differently depending on relative speed. Experimental confirmations came only later (and it is so hard actually to observe this phenomenon that there are still just a few). Equipped only with an active imagination—some of his teachers would no doubt have said *overactive*—Einstein began a revolution in physics that transformed our world.

car. All fine ideas. A *perfect* solution, however, would be a lot more dramatic. What if we did not need keys at all? Or what if we had the equivalent of keys that somehow we *couldn't* misplace—say, if they were part of our bodies?

Notice that here, already, right at the start, we have pushed ourselves entirely beyond questions like how to make our keys a little harder to lose. Instead, we are thinking about new kinds of keys or different practices that don't require keys at all. Combination locks? Voice-recognition systems, fingerprints, even some kind of bodily imprinting? Hiring a guard?

MIX AND MATCH

Many of today's familiar products are combinations of things not originally put together. Pencils didn't originally have erasers. Someone imagined putting them together—or perhaps accidentally just put them together—and now the eraser has become so much a part of the pencil that we don't even mention it anymore. Clock radios, toaster ovens, chocolate-chip cookies, umbrella strollers—all are inventions-by-combination.

Aspiring inventors can use the same method. Pick any two things at random and, well, put them together. Mix and match. Brainstorm from there. By way of illustration, I am going to try it right now, at my desk. Let's see. . . .

Postcards and a disk drive? OK, what about a postcard that you could mail to friends to put in their computers for pictures or a video and some words from you?

A wristwatch and a little flowerpot? What about wearable fresh-flower holders—a new kind of jewelry? Or flowers genetically engineered to change color on the hour?

A stapler and a houseplant? I don't know . . . sometimes it doesn't work! (What do you think?)

For more targeted problem-solving, take your problem, or some part of it, and do something similar: "mix" in some quite dissimilar objects or images and see whether some useful hybrid might suggest itself.

Your problem is finding buried landmines in former war zones? Mix in, say, flowers. It turns out that researchers are already at work on certain varieties of flowers that grow fast and nearly anywhere and change color near the distinctive chemical signatures of landmines.

Your problem is how to power wells in villages without electricity? In a recent World Bank development newsletter, I read of a project in rural Africa to power the pumps by hooking them to merry-go-rounds in schoolyards. I suppose one group of villagers was laboriously figuring out a way to power a pump and another group was finally getting some equipment for the playground. They put their needs together and devised a lovely way of meeting both at once. The kids pump water while playing!

More challenging but sometimes more powerful is to try the same thing with *analogies*. That is, take any problem and ask, "How is it *like* X?" where X is some other situation or idea or object. Again, it will seem awkward and strange at first, and often nothing will come of it. But startling new ways of thinking can also emerge. People had been using presses to get the juices out of grapes for centuries before Gutenberg applied the same process to printing—but no one else had made the connection.

Take the recycling issue again. By way of illustration, let us try a few random analogies. This time I'll go to the day's newspaper and again pick with reckless abandon and no pre-filtering.

Opera? That is, could the recycling issue somehow be *like* opera? Well, operas are musical, obviously. So maybe we need some good recycling music (real music, I mean, not just cheap jingles). Perhaps even a whole new musical style could be associated with recycling?

Religion? That is, how could recycling somehow be *like* a religious act? Maybe churches should start serving as recycling centers. Or maybe recyclable containers should be made so precious (that is, "sacred" in a sense) that no one would want to throw them away in the first place?

Making tea? I wonder if recycling could somehow be *like* responding to a teapot's whistle? So . . . could a recyclable item somehow "whistle" when it needed to be recycled or was being put into the wrong bin? Silly? Well, maybe it shouldn't

TARGETING YOUR QUESTIONS

On some problems it helps to set up your creative challenge with some analytical thinking up front. Define the problem carefully. Then clearly outline a good (or perfect!) solution and what means might produce it. *Then* start looking around for specific new ideas.

Case in point: sometimes I challenge my students to invent a completely new kind of clock, a device for telling time that has never been used before. To make any kind of clock, you need to harness some kind of process that occurs over a regular length of time, like the movement of the sun over a day or a pendulum through one of its swings. When you brainstorm ideas for a new kind of clock, you could target your search on identifying and making use of processes of this sort.

Dripping water, for instance: could you build a clock that tracks time by dropping water levels? Sure—drip clocks were common in the ancient world.

What else? Pulse, maybe? But pulse is variable. Keep thinking, though. Is variability necessarily a problem? Maybe you could think of it the other way around: a pulse-based timekeeper would give you "personal" time. Maybe you could even market a pulse-clock as a health aid. ("Is your time going by too fast?")

And are there new ways to use the familiar time cycles in the world, such as the sun's movement? Sundial wristwatches?

Certain possibilities come up, in short, because you are asking a targeted question. Of course, even in this kind of case, don't leave your wilder and wider-gauged methods aside. Do some random association too, maybe. (*Plants?* What about those flowers genetically engineered to change color on the hour?) Defining the problem itself can be a creative act. Just bear in mind that sometimes narrowing down a problem can take you a long way toward focused new ideas.

make noise, but it could make *some* sort of "statement." How about visually? Now there's an idea: maybe we could color-code recyclable items—say some strong shades of green—so you can tell at a glance that they are recyclable (in fact, even before you buy them) and whether you (or someone else) are

WAYS TO MULTIPLY OPTIONS—SUMMARY
• *Exotic Association.* Use random words, images, or other prompts or associations as provocations, and go from there. • *Go Public.* Ask around, brainstorm. • *Compare and Contrast.* Explore how the same problem is treated in other places and at other times. • *Exaggerate.* Go to extremes; work backward from "perfect" solutions. • *Mix and Match.* Try unexpected combinations and analogies.

putting them in the right or wrong bin. Far better than the current system of hard-to-read and harder-to-interpret numeric codes.

I like that last idea especially. Notice that we used several of this chapter's methods to arrive at it: we started with an analogy, then used "intermediate impossible" (could a recyclable item somehow "whistle" when it needed to be recycled?), then free-associated from there. It took a little time, but I think the result is quite fine.

FOR PRACTICE ◈

1. To make creativity second nature, rehearse these methods all the time, even just to occupy your spare moments or while you are driving with your friends or family in the car. Make a game of it, a daily practice, a routine. Use them to come up with five new murder mystery plots—every day. (How do you think the great mystery writers do it?) Sit down with a sheet of paper and use them to invent a better mousetrap. (Seriously—why not? You think it can't be done?) When you finish your newspaper in the morning, pick out two different topics or stories, even advertisements, and "mix and match." (What do you get? Ideas for new products? An unexpected solution to one of the world's pressing problems? That mousetrap you were working on?)

2. Mousetraps aren't the only things needing improvement. Use the methods in this chapter to think about how all manner of every-day and familiar things might be improved.

Clothes, for example: my students have proposed things like spray-on clothes; clothing in small pieces that you could snap together for different outfits; clothing that can double as other things, such as bags, seat covers. What about money? Designer money, for more interesting designs? Plastic coins? Paying sales taxes in some lump-sum way so as not to always have to deal with odd totals and making change?

Any clever ideas for making driving more efficient? Right-hand turns on red are still a fairly new innovation. One-way tollbooths only got their start in the 1970s. What a revolutionary idea: instead of paying a toll both ways, the motorist pays only one way, but twice the toll, reducing traffic jams and halving the expense of maintaining tollbooths. And all that time we old-timers put up with the both-way toll without realizing how inefficient it was! So what other possibilities are out there now, likewise right in front of our eyes?

Do you want to be an entrepreneur? Driving down a commercial strip one day, I started thinking about those quick-change oil and lube joints (like Jiffy Lube) and wondering what other goods and services could be offered on a "jiffy" basis. Jiffy Floss? Jiffy Brain Surgery? These are just funny. Others might be (semi)serious business opportunities. Jiffy Makeover? What about Jiffy School? "Just in time" education, like "just in time" parts deliveries in manufacturing. Education only when you need it—a joke or a whole new franchise?

Related to exaggeration is the method of *reversing* certain features of a problem. Other business opportunities might arise in this way. If we don't like sitting on hold for fifteen minutes waiting for an airline or bank representative to get to our phone calls (as if), consider reversing the situation. What if *they* called *us* back when they were ready to talk? This would be easy to arrange with current phone technology. Or again, ordinarily airlines or hotels or other sellers name their price and the rest of us decide whether the service is worth it to us at the stated price. Priceline.com creatively reversed the formula: instead, *we* name our price and the companies decide whether to take us up on it or not. Among some people it has become wildly popular—and the idea could go a lot farther, too. Adapt it.

3. Go back to the category of small but troublesome daily challenges introduced in the last chapter's exercises: boredom, too much TV, uncivil drivers, etc. You now have a much larger set of creative methods. Take up some of those problems again and generate more ideas using your new tools. (And again, keep your notes.)

Lack of cheap travel options, for instance: I'd be willing to bet that in half an hour with two friends, if you work hard and use the methods in this chapter, you could come up with three great new ways to travel the world virtually free—and that one of those ideas could probably make your fortune.

Here are a few further problems in the same category.

- Getting up in the morning—yourself or your friends or family. (This is a lovely little challenge, actually, with all sorts of unsuspected but thoroughly enjoyable options.)
- "Empty nest syndrome." (Maybe you college students are not thinking about this, but I bet your parents are.)
- Shoplifting.
- Inappropriate cell-phone use.
- Bad weather when you don't need it.
- Ways to improve your classroom. Very modest changes might make a dramatic difference. For example, instead of raising your hand when you have something to say, what if the rule were the opposite—that you have to raise your hand when you *don't*? What do you think the results would be? Why don't you try it?

4. Here is a sampling (just a sampling) of large-scale social, political, and technological design issues for you. Approach them with the same creative tools.

- Cars. Hybrid cars use a mix of electric and gas power and reroute braking energy to recharge the battery. Cars powered by hydrogen fuel cells are on the horizon. After half a century of fine-tuning the streamlining on the topsides, car designers are even paying attention to their undersides, which can benefit just as much from lower air resistance. So what else might be possible? If you were a car designer wanting to do your bit for ecology as well as style, what might you do?

- It's not only social conservatives who object to the content of so many TV programs: sex, violence, sensationalism-as-news, endless commercials. What else could TV be? Sure, we can put on "serious" or well-meaning shows, educational shows, or Mayberryish stuff. You can get a lot more creative than that. Give TV time to different artists to do what they will with it, maybe. If you were such a one, what would you do with it?

- Our children's, maybe even our own, moral and personal role models tend to be movie stars, athletes, political leaders (?). Who might be more suitable? More specifically, what more suitable role models might also have the allure and the visibility of the movie star, etc.? Might we have to create them? How?

- One-parent families have a tough time in contemporary society. Large and often unfair burdens on the parent (usually mother) also produce tensions for everyone. Certainly one option is to try to help the original parents to stay together (and to make better choices of partner in the first place). What other options might you suggest? Could some of them also help out other struggling families—say, with two working parents?

- Only three countries in the world have not adopted the metric system (kilometers, milligrams . . .) for measurements: Liberia, Myanmar, and the United States of America. Is this a problem? If so, what could be done about it?

- Americans' interest in politics continues to decline. But the stakes get ever higher. Maybe we should hold elections on a day when most people are free—or maybe, instead, give ourselves election day off? How about making election day a holiday—fireworks, parades leading to polling stations, the works? How about designating a special day one or two weeks before each election that voters spend discussing the issues, maybe even getting a small stipend to do so? How about forming a new political party to promote creative problem-solving on social problems?

- Oh, and while you're at it, can you devise some more constructive (less negative and divisive) forms of political protest?

4

BUILDING ON YOUR BREAKTHROUGHS

Suppose now that you have used some of the tools from the last chapters to good effect and you've arrived at an exciting and genuinely *new* idea about a problem that everyone else (maybe you too a minute ago) thought was thoroughly stuck.

Don't stop now! Our single greatest temptation is to stop as soon as we make a first breakthrough, as if some sort of final exam has been passed and now there is nothing more to be done. In fact we have usually only taken the first step of what could be many more. We've only cracked open the door. Real creativity only *begins* with the first breakthrough. Walk through that door—and keep going.

NEXT STEPS

How do you develop and deepen an idea once you make the initial breakthrough? Here are some ways.

1. Consider the practical challenges to implementing your idea, and then develop your idea to meet them. Ask yourself where problems and objections are likely to come up. For example, if you want to decrease litter by making containers so appealing that people won't throw them out, how will you do this? Make them refillable? Create a lucrative resale market? Maybe make them usable as building materials or toys? All perfectly good ideas, but still only beginnings; you can fill them out farther.

2. Refine your original idea by making it more specific. Clarify key terms; figure out ways to put your idea into effect; creatively apply it to a specific situation. For example, if you want to promote recycling by creating some good recycling jingles, what would be a good way to do this? Maybe it would be fun (and exactly appropriate) to "recycle" bits of music we already know?

3. Ask yourself where you might go next with your idea or suggestion. Starting from the idea of edible wrappers, for example, what should they taste like?

4. Add onto your first creative breakthrough with other creative ideas about the same problem. Go right back to the tools in the previous chapter to continue generating ideas, but now with the thought that your new ideas might be combined with your current one to make something still more creative.

5. Add onto your first creative breakthrough with other creative ideas about a *different* problem. Once again, this has a "random" feel, but (like all the exotic-association methods) it also can produce some wild and completely unexpected con-

nections. Try it almost mechanically: just take your problem and randomly select another problem—any problem at all—to see if there might be some cross-fertilization. Stick with it a while, even (in fact, especially) if it seems totally unpromising.

6. Extend your creative solution to other, similar problems. Barry Nalebuff and Ian Ayres call this "solutions in search of problems." If you have a great idea about one thing, don't leave it there—ask where else it could apply. Edible wrappers, for example, or rather the idea of eating things we currently throw away. The natural next question is, "What other throwaways could be made edible too?" Newspapers? For dogs, anyway? Pens? Schoolkids already chew their pens when taking tests; how about adding flavor and making the casing taste like popcorn or bubblegum? For adults, maybe add caffeine?

TWO IDEAS TO BUILD ON

Here are two problems that I regularly pose to my students and that are upcoming concerns on their minds. Both involve marriage. One is the amazing fact that almost half of new American marriages now fail within seven years. The amount of unhappiness involved is staggering. What can be done to help more marriages succeed?

There's also the smaller but nagging problem of *naming* when married. Currently, many women are expected to give up their original name for their partner's. As a result, though, the woman loses a part of her identity—a loss, and an unequal result too. Some women keep their original names when married. But this has other problems: it slights, perhaps, the new, shared identity. Hyphenating names is a more egalitarian approach, but it often produces unpronounceable results and anyway can't be carried on into the next generation. Couldn't we invent a better system?

About the naming problem, one idea my students often suggest is that marrying people choose their own, new, shared last name. That way they would share a name after all, and not an unmanageable name like "Van de Bodegraven-Ringelstetter" either.

About the relationship/divorce problem they have multiple ideas. One is that people should get to know each other better before getting married. This, my students say, should help people identify weakness or incompatibility with potential spouses before actually tying the knot.

These are both good ideas—already a large step beyond the culture that usually tells us there is really nothing to be done. Each is the kernel of a good suggestion, a creative idea. But each of these ideas, in truth, is also really only a starting point. Each of them needs a fair amount of development to be practical, and could be far more powerful if we build on it in some of the ways just outlined. Let's try.

TOWARD BETTER MARRIAGES

Take the "get to know your partner better" idea first. Let us first try to make the initial idea more specific. How could it be put into practice?

A natural suggestion might be to change the marriage laws to add the requirement that couples cannot marry until they have known each other for, say, at least a year. This should cut down on hasty marriages and eliminate the pressure some young people feel to marry right away if a relationship feels right. The cultural message would be to slow down, take your time, make sure this is the right person. It takes time.

Good so far. But questions arise again—and considering them systematically is, remember, another way to "go farther." One question is, "How could such a rule be enforced?" How could you prove you'd known each other long enough? Besides, many couples in marriage-like relationships (what the Australians call "de facto" marriage) don't in fact get legally married, but breaking up can be just as hard. Maybe we need something more than, or different from (just?) changing the marriage laws.

In class one day, a student group was stuck at this point. Yes, yes, they agreed, people really should get to know their prospective spouses better before getting hitched, but how could we really promote or enforce this? Hmm ...

I suggested bringing in ideas from somewhere else—whatever ideas might turn up. Since other groups were working on the marriage issue too, we turned to theim for some quick provocations. "We need a few random prompts—*please!*"

One group was thinking about how couples and families sometimes get too self-involved—that people don't do enough community service. They were thinking about adding incentives for people to help more outside the family unit. OK, then, specifically: could an idea about "more service" somehow go together with the idea about "getting to know you before marriage"?

At first glance, no: they are two separate ideas. But wait a minute ... What about community service as, essentially, a *way* of getting to know a potential spouse? That is, the idea would be to do the service work *together*. After all, getting to know someone is not just a matter of time. You could spend a year having delightful dates and vacations but have no clue whatsoever what your potential spouse is like under pressure, at work, or with children. To really get to know someone, you need to see and interact with that person in less ideal settings and under stress.

There you have it, then: people should be encouraged to do community service work together as a way not just of doing some good in the community but also of checking out a potential spouse. Being totally absorbed in each other is nice when you're in love, but it doesn't help much in getting ready to have children or to build working lives together. Service work is a way to be absorbed together in something bigger. Think of the enormous benefit to community service organizations—soup kitchens, environmental clean-ups, you name it—if large numbers of good-hearted young people made a practice of helping out. And think of the long-term benefits if people associated this kind of work with *romance*! Think of all the bad marriages prevented and good marriages cemented in this way.

By the way, this proposal also resolves another of the problems that came up about the original suggestion, which is how to prove that you and your partner have in fact known each other for the requisite year (or whatever period your new rules might require). This would be easy if there were records for community service.

WHAT'S IN A NAME?

About the naming problem, remember, one idea that might arise is that marrying people choose their own, new, shared name. Let us now try to take this idea a few steps farther too.

The initial idea is that when two people get married they would no longer be, say, John Smith and Maria Fuentes but John X and Maria X, where X is the new common name they choose. How interesting! Now, what would this look like in practice?

Certainly it would be a more egalitarian system, and it gives people a chance to be creative in naming themselves. On the down side, married people would no longer share any names with their parents or other birth-family members—possibly a problem, though on the traditional naming system this is already true of most married women. We also presume, I guess, that children would take X as their last name.

How can we develop this idea? For one thing, we might ask if there is some way we could have both the advantages of the new system—spouses readily sharing a name and getting to name themselves—with at least some of the advantages of the traditional way, such as sharing at least some names across generations. People do come to identify with their original names. It would be nice to have a naming system that allowed everyone a little more continuity.

Might we wonder if a better solution would be for married people to hold onto their original name while adding a new married name (that is, rather than simply changing names)? Actually, this would not be hard to do: their married name could become their new last name and their original last name could become their middle name, John Smith and Maria Fuentes would become John Smith X and Maria Fuentes X. And the kids would simply be Manuel or Maxine X.

This is a nice suggestion, a big step forward. It accomplishes more of what we want: everyone would still share a name with both parents, and parents with children; spouses would share a (single!) name with each other. It asks no more of a name change—in fact, it asks less—than most women are asked now.

Before we stop, though, we ought to ask whether we can do still better. (Again, take your time, don't stop too soon.) What other options are there? Once you ask the question this way, it becomes clear that there is at least one other alternative. Couples could also take a new married name as a *middle* name, while retaining their original last name. John Smith and Maria Fuentes would become John X Smith and Maria X Fuentes—the kids could still be Manuel or Maxine X.

Is this a better idea? Maybe, maybe not. It would take more getting used to. We are prone to add new names at the end and not in the middle of our original names. By the same token, though, it would be less disruptive. People would keep their original names but just expand them a little, and could choose to use their married middle name in some settings but perhaps not all, just as we do now with our middle names. As a parent at school relating to my kids, I might use only my middle (married, family) name, the name I share with them. At work, mostly, my original name might be enough. This scheme still allows people to share a name with both their spouses and their children, and with (both) their parents, with the additional advantage that they can keep their names upon marriage.

We do not need to decide between these options here. More important is simply to recognize them—and in particular that a more subtle but perhaps somewhat preferable option easily could be overlooked if we fasten too quickly onto the more obvious last-name option. Give it time.

FOR PRACTICE ◈

1. Design a completely new game or sport. For example, try to create a highly participatory new sport with environmental learning chiefly in mind. That is, create a game that not only gets people outdoors but encourages—even requires—the players to pay careful attention to nature, to understand more about ecology and the complexities of the larger world than they did before. Make it open to players of a variety of ages and levels of physical ability (maybe also to varied numbers of players?) but also interesting and challenging to players who want to be quite physically active. You'll need a variety of roles. Something like Capture the Flag, maybe? Spread it out over the land (some version of Hide and Seek, or how about some game with hidden treasure?), and ideally, make it playable in a variety of places, rather than requiring a dedicated playing field or special equipment.

Ultimately you'll need a specific and complete set of rules. Take your time, though: start with your general goals, make your game *really good* (why would people want to play it? where's the excitement?), keep the rules as simple and minimal as possible, etc.

Of course, there are all sorts of other games with other goals that you might also choose to invent. See if you can create something really different, though—for example, not another game with balls and goals or nets—but still a game that has the excitement and the challenge of ball games.

2. Design a completely new business. Begin by identifying a real need that is not now being met. Maybe it is a need that could not have been met in the past because the technology did not exist, or maybe it is even a very simple need that no one noticed or imagined a way to meet before. That idea will be your breakthrough— but again, it is only a beginning. Now design a business to meet the need you have identified. Again you will need a detailed, worked-out plan. Exactly what good or service will you offer? How will you market it? How can you be sure that your product cannot be co-opted by other companies or even offered free by others?

You may know that Federal Express was conceived in a Yale Business School class with exactly this assignment. One-day package delivery was barely imaginable in 1965—according to legend, the professor actually flunked the project!—but FedEx was launched in 1971 with immediate success, and today serves practically the entire globe with a $30 billion annual income. So again, what's next?

You could even connect your new business with some of the ideas in this chapter about marriage. For example, if people add a new middle or last name, how would they pick that name? Are there new jobs here for naming consultants and companies?

3. The exercises for the last chapters put before you a wide range of problems and challenged you to make some creative break-throughs with each one of them. I also asked you to keep your notes on your ideas. Now go back to your initial ideas on those problems and *go farther,* using the methods laid out and modeled in this chapter. Keep notes on your new ideas as well.

Though you have a whole range of problem areas to choose from, best might be to start from some of your previous ideas that you like the most. Clever ideas about getting up in the morning? New travel options? Ways to reimagine TV programming or national politics? Or—god forbid—school?! After you've worked on these questions again, compare your developed set of ideas to your original list of ideas from the last chapters. I am sure you had some terrific ideas on that list, but do you see now how much farther you can go?

Here is one more challenge: can you think of new and practical ways to generate electricity from ocean tides or waves? A few ideas have been proposed—damming a bay, for example, letting the tides fill it, and then closing the dam and letting the water run out through turbines at low tide—but they tend to be usable only in a few coastal areas. What else might be possible? Or again, can you think of better ways to capture wind power than building windmill farms (which have their own environmental costs) in particularly windy places? How about other ways to generate power—perhaps from sources right around us that we don't recognize yet? Again, work out a plan. Figure out the details, on both the technological and the business sides.

4. Problem-solving methods address, of course, *problems.* But creativity can go farther still. Why wait until something becomes a problem before trying to make creative improvements? Everything can be creatively improved all the time. In particular, when we have a good solution to one problem, why not try to extend it to others? Remember again the last of the means of "building on your break-throughs": extending your creative solutions to other, quite different problems.

Barry Nalebuff and Ian Ayres give some lovely examples. Coffee shops have appeared in bookstores, for instance—why not in public libraries? (Actually, a few big-city libraries now have them.) Or again, black boxes in airplanes store data about all crew actions, speeds, forces on the plane, etc., and so are crucial to understanding what goes wrong when planes crash. Why not build in similar data storage for cars? No more squabbling about the actual causes of accidents, no more uncertainty about product defects (was the driver's foot on the accelerator or the brake, etc.?)—the data would be there. In fact, it turns out, the data already *are* there, in various computer monitors already in our cars. The information just needs to be more downloadable (and stored in a "hardened" way to protect it in crashes). Moreover, in Europe, where such devices are being tested, they turn out to make drivers much safer as well. Some taxi fleets have seen collisions decrease by two-thirds. Imagine parents being able to review their teenager's driving download when the kid brings the family car home. Imagine even building in warning signals when a driver is exceeding safe driving levels. (Why stop with merely recording bad driving? Any device that can monitor these levels can also synthesize your mother's voice telling you to slow down.)

The Mormons assign every church member two other members to look after, so that every member is also looked after themselves by two other members. Couldn't that kind of practice be usefully extended?

OK, your turn . . .

5

REFRAMING PROBLEMS

Now I have some news that may surprise you. Sometimes there are better ways to address problems—better ways to take them up, to move into and beyond them—than "solving" them in the straightforward ways we have so far considered. "Solving" them is not always the most creative response.

So some major steps remain to be taken in our quick survey of the realm of creativity. This chapter introduces three alternative ways of addressing problems.

THINK LATERALLY

A straight line is not always the best way between two points. What if there were a steep wall or an unfriendly dragon in the way? Rather than just charging directly ahead into a problem, then, we also need to look for sidesteps and end runs. We need to mentally revisit every part of a problem, not just the one or two seemingly most obvious. Each aspect can be varied, questioned, stretched. This is what de Bono calls "lateral thinking."

A group of friends were swimming together in a creek when suddenly one of them became tangled in some underwater vines. Struggling desperately, he was still not able to get to the surface; he remained a foot under. His friends dove again and again to try to untangle him, but it quickly became clear that they could not get him free in time.

One friend thought: if he can't get to the air, maybe the air can … get to *him*? Right on shore was a homeowner with a garden hose and pruning shears. Two snips later there was a two-foot length of hose. He had a makeshift snorkel! The trapped swimmer was saved by a friend who shifted her attention to an aspect of the problem that was more easily solved. He literally owes his life to lateral thinking.

Remember the well-known story about the ancient scientist Archimedes. The king of the day had given his metalsmith a certain amount of gold to make a crown. The king came to suspect, though, that the smith took some of the gold for his own enrichment and substituted silver instead. Archimedes got the job of finding out.

If Archimedes knew the volume of the crown, he could take an equal volume of solid gold and weigh the two against each other: if the crown came out lighter, he'd know it was partly silver. But here was the rub: how could he measure the volume of something so lacey and finely worked? He could hardly just melt it back down—and calculation would take a lifetime. What to do?

Legend has it that Archimedes went to the public baths one day, this problem weighing on his mind, and at the moment of lowering himself into one of the tubs, water splashing over

LATERAL THINKING AND THE MARS LANDERS

Suppose you are a NASA engineer designing spacecraft to land on the surface of Mars. The problem is that the Martian surface is rocky in many places, and a lander that came down on a boulder field could easily tip over or get wedged between rocks, damaging the craft and making it impossible to deploy solar panels or antennas— and there is $500 million down the drain. It's happened.

Mission planners try to select landing spots that are level and rock-free, but you never know (and besides, sometimes the rougher regions are the ones they want to explore). Landers can land "softly" (that is, fire rockets on the way down to lower themselves gently to the surface, though this takes a lot of complexity and fuel, adding weight and cost), but they still have to land on their own, rocks or no. Mars is way too far away for remote-controlled landings.

Can you think of any lateral solutions? Try it. Instead of trying to make landings "softer," why not try to make the lander better able to land "hard"—that is, a lot better cushioned? Good—that could solve half the problem. But there is still the problem of finding a more or less level site. Artificial intelligence? Maybe, but only at immense extra cost, weight, and uncertainty. Keep at it. Aren't there any *dumb* methods for finding a level site?

Surely there are. Just let a beach ball go in a big yard and it will find a level site all by itself. All you need is gravity and a little time. Hmm . . . interesting analogy, huh?

Two rovers arrived on Mars in early 2004 mounted inside, well, huge inflatable beach balls. They were slowed in their approach through the Martian atmosphere first by retrorocket and then by parachute, but they arrived on the surface by being dropped from the chute from several hundred feet and then—yes—bouncing along the surface (big time: up to 50–60 feet on the bounces, apparently) until they rolled to a stop, after which the "balls" deflated and the rovers were ready to explore.

The latest is that NASA may extend the beach ball concept to design the next generation of rovers too. Instead of using a golf cart-like powered rover, the idea is to design something that the

Martian winds themselves could blow around, like tumbleweed or balloons or, again, beach balls. This idea, by the way, was first suggested by a local sixth-grade science class, collaborating with a North Carolina State University engineering class under contract with NASA. All going to show that while creative thinking is certainly not rocket science, rocket science can certainly use creative thinking! And when you're stuck, ask a sixth-grader.

the sides, he found his "lateral" solution. The volume of any solid object equals its displacement in water. He could measure it indirectly. All he needed to know was how much water the crown displaced. This was the occasion, supposedly, of Archimedes running home naked—too excited to put on his clothes—shouting "Eureka!" ("I have found it!") at the top of his lungs.

Modern scientists face similar challenges, and lateral thinking continues to offer unexpected solutions. Astronomers suspect that planets orbit other stars, for instance, but they're extremely difficult to see in even the best telescopes. Their light is very dim, and they are massively outshone by their suns. The solution: look not for the planets themselves but for the wobble their gravity causes in their star's movement. Again, indirection. Archimedes would be proud.

THE PROBLEM IS THE OPPORTUNITY

Paul Wellstone was an unknown political science professor in Minnesota when he ran for the U.S. Senate against a powerful incumbent. Wellstone had very little money—usually the kiss of death in a statewide political campaign. But his campaign managed to make an *advantage* of his very lack of money. They created extremely short TV ads featuring Wellstone talking *very fast* about key issues—getting his positions out, of course, but even more importantly highlighting the fact that the other guy had all the money. People laughed, and got the point. Wellstone went on to win and to a distinguished career in the Senate.

We label situations as "problems" when something comes up that threatens to disrupt or complicate the plans we are following. But this very label can be a trap, blinding us to the possibilities in those very problems. Maybe the problem instead, like Wellstone's lack of money, is an *opportunity*. Instead of trying to get rid of such "problems," in short, we should ask how we can make use of them. This is a second method for reframing problems. Call it *opportunism*.

Take Chapter 1's buried rock one more time. First we wanted to move the rock. Then we wanted to move the house—that's the lateral step. But finally we decided to use the rock to build a better house. The rock itself turned out to be not a problem but a *solution*, an opportunity to create (redesign) a far better and truly fabulous house using the rock itself for a dramatic wall.

A 99% Hispanic community in south Texas was told again and again that their nearly total reliance on Spanish was a problem and a weakness. But a group of students, backed by some community organizations, cast it differently. Here is a school that is nearly all Spanish-speaking. Is that something unremittingly terrible, they asked? Couldn't anyone see some advantages in this very situation?

Well, yes, they said. Ask the question this way, and the answer is "Of course." In other schools around the country, kids are desperate to learn Spanish. We know that "immersion" is a good way to do this. And, like any language, Spanish is learned best when accompanied by Spanish culture. So why not use this very school for Spanish-immersion teaching?

Certainly there are enough "teachers," since every kid can help. This idea has now grown into a full-scale program with classes, visits to local Hispanic community events, and even trips to Mexico, staying with host families with ties to the Texas school.

Many environmental issues lend themselves to opportunistic rethinking too. Recycling, for example. In nature, what's waste for one species is resource for the next. Trees make use of the carbon dioxide we exhale, as we make use of the oxygen they exhale. So couldn't we begin to think that way about the massive waste in our own system? Why not look at trash as a kind of raw material?

Building materials account for 40% of landfill volume in the United States right now. Why not recycle them into new construction and, from now on, make building materials to be easily recycled? Or again, power plants create "excess" heat, which usually is dissipated into the air or water, often at great cost. But couldn't that heat be used for something? How about home heating? There you have the origins of "cogeneration," in which power companies also market hot water to surrounding communities—not incidentally reducing the cost of both power and heat.

TRY PREVENTION

Everyone knows that it's better to stay healthy than to wait until you get sick and then have to deal with the illness. We don't always act on this knowledge, but we do know it. Taking daily vitamins is a lot wiser than waiting until you get a cold and then pulling out the decongestants and throat lozenges (and suffering anyway). Folk wisdom knows it too, as in the saying "An ounce of prevention is worth a pound of cure" or "A stitch in time saves nine."

TWO PROBLEMS, ONE SOLUTION

When Henry Ford was setting up the first assembly lines to build the Model T, his suppliers got very specific requests about how to build the boxes in which they sent their bolts or cushions. A certain kind of wood had to be used, cut to certain sizes, with holes drilled just in certain places. Puzzled, but anxious for Ford's business, they complied.

It turned out that once the boxes were unpacked at the assembly line, they were taken apart and used for the Model T's floorboards. They were already cut and drilled in just the right ways.

Ford *could* have posed "the" problem simply as, "How do we get rid of excess boxes?" No one would have seen the box as anything but litter. Instead, Ford asked, "What could the box be used for?" Instead of becoming litter, the excess box material then became an opportunity. Ford was able to take two problems—procuring floorboards and getting rid of unwanted boxes—and turn them into one solution. Reuse (or "next use") was planned into the very design of things. Some thinkers now call this "precycling." We could use a lot more of it.

This same way of thinking can be a form of creativity as well. The strategy is the same. Think preventively, "proactively." Don't just take the problem for granted—ask whether it even needs to come up in the first place. Look to its causes. What is the problem *behind* the problem, so to speak? Is there a way to rearrange things so that we don't get stuck with this problem, or anything like it, at all? How, at least, can we keep it from coming up so often and/or in so difficult a form?

Here is a little piece I saw in the newspaper:

Recently a mother complained to me that her 9-year-old daughter watches television for eight hours a day and she couldn't get her to stop. "Why not?" I asked. "Because," the woman answered, "the TV is in her bedroom."

You can imagine the usual parent–child fights. You can even imagine other creative solutions, like rewards for keeping the TV off or agreed weekly viewing schedules. But best of all, obviously, would just be to take the TV out of her room. What's striking is that *this* solution apparently never even crossed the mother's mind. Sometimes we need help to think proactively, it seems.

A decade or so ago, everyone was embroiled in deep debates over what to do when people ended up brain-dead but physically still alive on hospital respirators. Families would plead to let them die, but the law wasn't clear and there were no moral precedents; so typically they were kept going, sometimes for years, breaking the family's bank as well as their hearts.

Probably in this kind of situation there is no good answer. In any case, we were not finding one. What changed since then is chiefly one thing: living wills. Now most people have declared themselves in advance on the subject, usually to say that they do not want to be kept alive in such a condition. The lawyers are satisfied, and the entire matter has calmed down immensely. "An ounce of prevention ..."

Fertility clinics are doing the same. When these clinics started storing couples' fertilized embryos, they found themselves in huge battles if couples split up. Which partner "owned" the embryos? We were headed right for a lot of head-shaking and decades of contentious cases winding their ways through the courts. The clinics, wisely, took a very different and preventive approach. Now, before they accept an embryo at all, they ask each couple to designate one or the other as the embryo's "owner" in the event of divorce. No more problem! (This is not even an ounce of prevention—more like a milligram—but it does the trick.)

Or take the problem of speeding once again. We've considered some unusual responses, such as putting flashing lights on top of speeding cars or spikes on the steering column. One thing we have not done, though, is to ask why people speed in the first place. Couldn't we also cut down on speeding by addressing or removing its *causes*? What would "prevention" look like here?

One precondition for speeding is that cars can go much faster than the speed limits. One ridiculously simple idea to cut down on speeding, then, would be to stop making cars that can go so fast, at least for very long. Or build in some speed-control system. A recent British study concludes that simple speed-limiting devices responding to GPS information and road-condition bulletins would reduce fatal accidents by 60% (that is, in the United States, it could save more than 25,000 lives a year).

The main reason I speed myself (of course very rarely) is being a little late for work. Once again, this readily suggests a few unexpected but totally logical means of prevention. Leaving for work a little earlier, for one. Likewise, I'd be less rushed if I simply scheduled my first class a little later.

And why not generalize this? For many jobs, we could institute a system of "flex-time," where work begins when you show up, rather than requiring you to show up at a set time. At one stroke this reduces the time pressures created by a rigid work schedule. People would no longer have to speed to arrive on time.

Notice once again that this is a different *kind* of problem-solving. We are no longer taking the problem as fixed and simply trying—however creatively—to cope. Now we are reframing "the" problem itself. Not surprisingly, then, other sorts of issues and advantages typically come up too. Another aspect of flextime worth considering, for instance, is that it evens out traffic and therefore cuts down on traffic jams (which are also a cause of speeding since they slow people down and create

---

WAYS TO REFRAME PROBLEMS—SUMMARY

The methods in this chapter ask you to rethink problems themselves as they are usually presented. How can they be redefined?
What are their causes? Are they necessarily even problems at all?

- *Think Laterally.* Survey all the outlying aspects of the problem
  in search of alternative approaches.
- *Find The Opportunities in the Problem.* "If life hands you a
  lemon, make lemonade!"
- *Try Prevention.* How can this problem be headed off before it
  even comes up?

---

impatience). Workplaces could encourage staggered schedules
for this reason. Likewise, flextime should cut down on the
demand for new roads, which are typically designed with peak
loads—rush-hour traffic—in mind, and therefore could save
millions of dollars in construction and maintenance costs.

FOR PRACTICE ❖

1. Here is a little list of everyday annoyances. Practice the tools
introduced in this chapter on them. In each case, ask yourself if
there is a way not so much to "solve" the problem exactly as it
stands but instead to reframe it—laterally, opportunistically, and/or
proactively—and, primarily, for yourself. (That is, what can *you* do
specifically about *this* situation?)

- Habitual lateness: your kids or yourself or someone you
  depend on repeatedly being late for school or work. Or getting
  up on time in the morning (if you find it difficult).
- Neighbors (upstairs, downstairs, next door) playing loud
  music at unfortunate hours of the day or night.
- Boredom. (You had some ideas about it in Chapter 2—now
  keep going. And what if you're mainly bored in school or at
  work?)

- Long, long waits in line (grocery stores, airport security check-points, Department of Motor Vehicles, etc.) or traffic jams.

- Weeds. Was Emerson right that a weed is just a plant we haven't figured out how to appreciate yet?

2. Here is a list of design issues—products and social arrange-ments—to approach in the same way. Use all your tools, of course, but especially those in this chapter.

- Can you figure out a way to make cars better able to get them-selves unstuck when they've slipped off the road or into a snowbank?

- Water heaters keep large amounts of water heated all the time, even though we use it only occasionally. When we do want hot water, on the other hand, sometimes we need more than the heater holds. "On-demand" water heaters solve both of these problems, but, not surprisingly, they use a lot of energy to instantly heat water, and you need several of them if you have several different points at which you need hot water. Design something better.

- Besides the weed problem, lawns (and public fields and golf courses) have huge water requirements, which in dry areas can eat up enormous amounts of precious water, as well as requir-ing undue herbicides and fertilizers. Another approach?

- There is a large and growing number of uninsured drivers—so many that we need to insure ourselves against them. What can be done?

- Our children's lives are too busy and too scattered. Soccer here, music lessons there, seeing some friends a 20-minute drive in yet another direction, etc. What to do?

- Future manned space missions. You know what manned space exploration has looked like so far. How might it look in the future? How might it be done dramatically better? (Just one hint: must the explorers come back?)

3. Here is a list of some major social problems. Begin by sketching for yourself the usual ways of approaching the problem: this will give you something to react against and try to move beyond. Use all your tools, but again concentrate on those in this chapter.

- Homelessness. Can you rethink this problem from the beginning?

- Suburban sprawl. Does it create unique city-planning opportunities as well as problems? Like what?

- We're becoming more conscious of the vulnerability of coastal construction (houses, roads) to hurricane damage (winds, washouts, storm surges). How else might we think about people living on and/or visiting our coasts and beaches? And are there alternative ways to build coastal cities?

- A fifth to a quarter of the U.S. population is obese. People aren't finding the time to exercise, and we eat badly too. New ideas?

- What might the elderly do with their time? How could society be restructured to respond to their needs and to better enable them to contribute? How about a system of adoptive grand-parents, as some of my students have suggested? And what other opportunities might aging represent? Must even selective memory loss necessarily be viewed as a mental failing? Could it even be regarded as an *advantage*? How could that possibly be?

- We say that drugs offer an escape from school or work or just life itself. But this only leads to other questions. Why do so many people need such an escape in the first place? What can we do about school or work or life itself so that such an escape is less tempting? Aren't there less lethal ways to make life joyful and interesting?

- Another drug issue: the "performance-enhancing" drugs used and abused by athletes. High school and even younger athletes risk their health for an unnatural edge; the World Anti-Doping Agency (great name, huh?) polices competitions such as the Olympics. Other competitors want to stay drug-free but to compete on a level playing field. Any other ways to approach all of this?

- As retribution for the most serious of crimes we tend to think of only the death penalty or life imprisonment. What other options might there be? How else might we approach the whole question of punishment and prison?

You might also take up any of the other issues you've considered in this book. Start with your notes from previous chapters—but here again, remember, the challenge is to *go farther,* using the new methods introduced in this chapter.

6

FULL-TIME CREATIVITY

By now I hope that you are thoroughly captivated by the possibilities for creative thinking. I want to conclude this book by painting a picture of creative thinking as a way of life.

CREATIVITY EVERY DAY

Look around you, right now, wherever you are. Maybe a schoolroom or library, maybe at home, maybe somewhere else. Take a good long look. Now ask yourself, "How can this room be improved?" Are there one or two changes that you can make *right now* that would markedly improve the space? Why not make them? New lamps, new colors on the walls? Murals? Opening the windows, changing the seating?

Anything is fair game. There are questions and possibilities every time you turn around. You're biking home, maybe? OK, that uncomfortable little bike-helmet strap under your chin—there has got to be a better way. Figure it out. The bumper-stickers on passing cars: could bikes have them too? (Where would they go? What shape would they have?) On a larger scale, how can your city be made more bikeable? (Dedicated bike trails, distinct from roads? Bike hours, when cars aren't allowed? What else?)

Maybe at a party you meet a person who leads dances for very old people at senior centers. He needs dances that people can do in wheelchairs or only with the top halves of their bodies. You could just smile and move on. You could also brainstorm right then and there. How about using some flags or streamers so that there is a dramatic sense of movement but without great physical demands? Hmm ... and what sorts of dances could perhaps *only* be done by 95-year-olds?

In the night: dreams. How could we remember our dreams better? What would it take? Training? What kind of training? Or maybe a different way of waking up in the morning? There are cultures in which dreams are so honored that the whole community will act them out the next day. Could we imagine sharing our dreams with family and friends, rather than just keeping them to ourselves or sharing them with psychiatrists?

In short, there is nothing mandatory about the way the world is right now. Everything is open to rethinking and change. Try to imagine how things *could* be, not just how they are. Wherever you are, and all the time. And follow through by making some actual changes. Dream notebooks, new bike helmets (another business opportunity)—whatever it might be. You've already seen that you can make serious creative progress on everyday problems, from getting up in the morning to making better marriages. Full-time creative people make a regular practice of it.

Besides, everyday creativity is also just plain fun. Coming up with new ideas is exciting even when they have no practical use whatsoever. That is why people like brain-teasers. Exotic association, brainstorming, mixing and matching, lateral thinking—this is not thinking-as-usual. There is a freshness and energy to it, a spring in your step.

Creative thinking is healthy too—literally. It's good for your brain. Scientists used to think that brain function gradually declines over one's whole life and that there is nothing much we can do about it. Now they think the opposite. Though some mental functions do gradually decline with time, others actually improve, at least until late old age; and—here's the key thing—almost all of them show less decline with more mental exercise. Circulation improves, new cells grow in. It's not enough to be physically active. You have to *think* hard too.

CREATIVE GOOD CITIZENSHIP

Creativity is also a social contribution. And it is not just that occasionally you may save a drowning swimmer or reenergize a stuck weather report. Think again of the many social problems we have tackled. Maybe by now you have found a completely new way of thinking about drugs, travel, school, TV programming, black boxes in cars, recycling, and on and on— and, again, you are equipped to find many more. Creative thinking along these lines can improve life for all of us.

Social creativity has its full-time requirements too. First of all, obviously, draw in other people. Practice creativity as visibly, explicitly, and invitingly as you can. Teach it to your children. Talk to people—to family, to friends, to students or teachers, to coworkers and colleagues, to elected officials. Talk to anyone who will talk back. *Someone* has to step up to creativity, to be the "idea person" in an organization or on the block. You've got the tools, why not you?

With the best of your new ideas, go public. Write letters to the editor of your local newspaper. Make constructive suggestions, rather than complaining or criticizing. Most newspapers are also happy to consider guest editorials—check your local paper's website for a link to the editorial page. People have even organized problem-solving shows on local radio stations. Callers phone in their problems, and the hosts brainstorm right on the air.

Go to meetings of your City Council or County Planning Commission (or PTA, Neighborhood Association, etc.). Probably you'll be surprised at how few other people show up on a regular basis. Just one person willing to speak up often can make a real difference. Don't hesitate to contact your representatives or other decision-makers (school principals, employers, etc.), either. Get some new ideas into circulation. Chapter 3 even proposed a new political party dedicated, first and foremost, to creative thinking in service of the common good.

Much of this may sound familiar. Really it's just plain old good citizenship with a creative edge. Yet I want to emphasize an aspect of it that is not so familiar: the power of creative thinking to *inspire* people. It's not very often that employers, say, or elected representatives hear from people with creative suggestions. Most people either just gripe or advocate some prepackaged position—and the vast majority never take part at all. But we're all drawn to new ideas, to the sense that even really tough problems have hopeful possibilities. And, most basically, people are drawn to the creative spirit that shows itself when a person starts to look for new ideas. Anyone whose attitude is more creative and promising will stand out—and then your ideas can go a long way.

THE GLOBAL IDEAS BANK

There are global organizations seeking out and featuring new ideas for bettering the world. One of my favorites is the Institute for Social Inventions, a British organization that runs a global website called the Global Ideas Bank (check them out at www.globalideasbank .org) and publishes collections of great ideas every few years with lovely titles like *The Book of Visions* and *Setting the World Alight*. Check out their website for literally thousands of great ideas and for links to other web resources.

The Global Ideas Bank defines a "social invention" as "a new or imaginative way of tackling a social problem or improving the quality of life," something that "changes the way in which people relate to themselves or each other, either individually or collectively." On the website you'll find ideas about teaching music to the (supposedly) "unmusical," self-constructed housing for the homeless, new kinds of childbirth and hospices (and other new forms of, well, dying), taxing TV violence, and on and on and on. The ideas about marriage and naming introduced in Chapter 4 of this book are also listed there, as well as more than fifty ideas on other topics, I'm proud to say, from my former students.

Anyone can submit an idea, though submissions are screened by the editors for originality and appropriateness and only the best make it to the books. There are even cash prizes for the year's best ideas. (Note that the Body Shop has a similar prize—in fact, they have a whole department of social innovation, as do many companies and workplaces: there are even jobs in this field!) There is no limit on how many submissions you may make, either (there are also prizes for people who have had the most ideas listed). Special efforts are made to get the best ideas into practice and to track the results. So . . . send those ideas in!

CREATIVITY TO CHANGE THE WORLD

Radical creativity can also *change the world*. It can be as practical as everyday creativity but thinks on a vastly larger scale—and does not shrink from even the wildest and most utopian hopes.

Take the car, for example. We have gone from a few curiosities putt-putting harmlessly around the back roads to 600 million–plus cars on the planet, dominating the city and the landscape, ruling economies, and even altering the climate. It is easy to despair over these truly massive problems. But the very fact that the car has become so dominant so quickly could also be read the other way around: as an encouragement to visualize the next big change. If such an absolutely dramatic change was possible in only a century (mostly in the last half-century, really), then, well, dramatic change is possible. Again. It's up to us to imagine the next one.

Already cars are being remade before our eyes. Clever high-school students spend an afternoon retrofitting their engines and then drive across the country on nothing but used vegetable oil—the exhaust smells like french fries. Hybrid engines radically improve mileage; fuel cell and hydrogen engines offer enormously improved efficiency and no emissions except water.

Better cars, though, are really only a temporary solution. Death and mayhem on the roads, traffic jams, highway costs and land loss, political and environmental harms—most of these problems would only get worse.

Alternatives to cars are on the way. South American and European cities are already limiting cars or banning them entirely and have built sparkling and efficient public bus or train systems with the savings from *not* having to pay for so many roads, wrecks, parking ramps, traffic cops, etc. Urban planners design high-density developments around new transit stops so that people can get to grocery stores and work and home in just a short walk from the stops.

Good so far, again—but we can go farther. What about "bike buses," say, that pick up bike riders from gathering spots, quickly transport them ten or twenty miles over high-speed tracks or roads, and then drop them off to efficiently disperse to wherever they are going? And what else? Shared neighborhood carpool vehicles? Safe hitchhiking systems? (Some are being developed.) New kinds of rickshaws?

But we still have not gotten as radical as we might. Suppose now that we go back to the very beginning and frame "the" problem in a different way. Rather than providing better cars or even better public transit, wouldn't it make more sense to reduce or eliminate the need for travel in the first place? Suppose people could stay home, stay in the neighborhood, most of the time. Shopping could be local again, as it was not so long ago, with corner groceries and farmer's markets complemented by the latest forms of Internet shopping for less commonly sought and durable goods. We could "tele-commute," shifting many jobs to local community centers like high-tech branch libraries or a neighborhood Internet café plus childcare centers, schools, gardens. (Sweden is already building such "tele-cottages" nationwide.) We could promote "virtual travel," maybe, and when we take actual, physical vacation trips, we could take them long and slow: walk, bike, take a camel.... Doesn't that sound like a better life?

Here are a few other radical ideas by way of going out with a bang.

We have come to recognize that we are all citizens of one Earth. Yet our politics are riven by national rivalries. If we are to have a truly global politics, must it be built on top of the nation-states? Maybe we should not even be thinking about a global order on the model of a government at all but more like, say, a *network*—a rich set of interconnections, contacts, and dialogues. And if that sounds familiar, it should. Could it be that an entirely new form of direct global politics is now possible through the Internet? Why are we not already e-mailing directly with Iraqis, Israelis, South Africans? How much would it take to create systematic, large-scale contacts of this sort? What might evolve from them? New kinds of global representatives, spokespeople, leaders?

Then there is the question of space. When humans finally take off for Mars, are they going to be the familiar all-human round-trip crew piloting a capsule and driven by burning Earth's fossils? It's not possible, actually: we can't send enough air and food to last the whole trip. Possibly not even enough fuel. What then? Might we have to rethink what space missions are, who goes on them—in fact, everything about them?

For starters, why not one-way trips? You think we couldn't find extraordinary people, maybe more the adventurer and the poet types, who'd be willing to ship out for good? It's a lot easier to drop people on planets than to get them back off.

The question of life support requires some rethinking too. Actually, a whole community of plants and animals must go, to replenish the air and provide food for each other and for the poor humans. A sort of Earth-in-miniature. How would such a craft look? How shall we think of it: more like an ark, maybe, than a capsule?

And what drives an ark? We are at the point of testing space probes that ride the solar winds: sailboats, in effect, to the stars. Others envision living forms—spacecraft *grown* rather than made, with trees bio-engineered inside-out, maybe, as epic poet and science fiction writer Frederick Turner imagines them, with a huge sealed central shaft sunlighting the forests and fields growing *in*.

And why *not* send life back out into the cosmos, even creating Earth-like atmospheres elsewhere, on Mars for example, which has enough gravity and atmosphere already and a good bit of water? What Mars needs is some serious global warming, which we're pretty good at, after all.

But enough. These are sweeping and sketchy ideas about very large issues. They are certainly not the only ideas or necessarily the best ideas. In the end, they might not even be good ideas. The main point is only that new and radically creative ideas are *possible*. And again, they will come from somewhere—why not us? If these are not to your taste—or even if they are—you know what to do. . . .

FOR PRACTICE ❖

1. Start noticing what needs to change—right next to you, and out in the larger world too. Make lists. Some of what you notice may suggest personal changes, some may open business opportunities, some may launch political campaigns. But the first step is to make a regular and systematic practice of paying attention.

One way to do so is to get yourself a nice, thick notebook and write down one problem area per page. Maybe commit yourself to add at least one page/problem each day. Later you may add more aspects of the problem or cross-reference other pages/problems. Then start making note of creative ideas too, of possible solutions. When the time is right, deliberately use the methods from this book to generate a lot more. Commit yourself to taking the best of these and putting them into practice and/or into the public discussion.

2. Here is a list of some of our biggest social challenges. Take them now as creative opportunities. Take your time and give them your best.

- How can we drastically reduce human impacts on natural environments? How can we wake up to nature before it is too late? Must environmentalism highlight only dangers and disasters? What about new holidays, new kinds of learning, new kinds of art even? What is the fundamental root of the environmental crisis, anyway?
- Problems of *work* include too much of it (the average work week is forty-four hours and climbing, and many people need

more than one job), work that is not fulfilling (*must* work be unpleasant? why? how can we be willing to spend so much of our best energy on merely getting by?), high unemployment rates (some people work too much and others can't find work at all: does this suggest any changes?), and the exporting of so many jobs to cheap and exploitative foreign factories. Can you envision any systematic way to address these problems?

- Why is *school* so universally disliked? *Must* it be so unpleasant? Why? Do we need so much of it? Could we do without it entirely? What could people do otherwise? (Do some comparing and contrasting. Look at some of the newest and most radical ideas about schools—and I don't mean just lengthening or shortening the school year a little or reducing class sizes by 2% or something.) What else is possible?

- Armies are good for fighting wars, not for building functioning societies on the ruins. We need a new organization that can move into war-ravaged and other damaged states and rebuild, indeed build *better*. What should it look like? Does it exist already in embryo? (Where?) What kinds of skills would such a "Reconstruction Force" call for? (Would it be a "Force" at all?) Who would join? (Think afresh here: it wouldn't have to be the young and most able-bodied.) How would it work? How would the participants be trained?

- What is real security? Keeping nasty people far enough away that they can't hurt us? Even if this were possible, isn't there more we might aspire to? And if it is *not* possible—not in the long run, not in an interconnected world—then, once again, what else might we aspire to? (Related: is there some alternative approach to *crime* that might make a dramatic difference? Could some criminal activity be rechanneled into something socially constructive? Is some so-called crime perhaps even socially constructive already—like, say, some graffiti? What about the fear factor, which often is way out of proportion to the actual dangers? Why? What can be done about this?)

3. Finally, here are some very large problems and problem areas that I am just going to name, and let you define the problems themselves as well as tackle the creative challenges they pose. Don't slight the definition part, for just shaping the questions involved is already a creative act. (So, for one thing, define them broadly and open-mindedly: leave maximum room for creative [re]thinking!) If there are multiple aspects to these problems (hint: there certainly are), make a list. Then pull out your tools for creative thinking.

Medicine and health

Terrorism

Community

Aging

Pollution

Population

Making the world more beautiful

Happiness

Take your time—give yourself time to take—and good luck!

NOTES AND SOURCES

FOR FURTHER READING

Extended introductions to creative thinking are Edward de Bono, *Serious Creativity* (HarperCollins, 1992) and *Lateral Thinking* (Harper, 1970); Barry Nalebuff and Ian Ayres, *Why Not? How to Use Everyday Ingenuity to Solve Problems Big and Small* (Harvard Business School Press, 2003); Charlie and Maria Girsch, *Inventivity* (Creativity Central, 1999); and Marvin Levine, *Effective Problem-Solving* (Prentice Hall, second edition, 1993). On proactive thinking, Stephen Covey's *The Seven Habits of Highly Effective People* (Simon and Schuster, 1990) is classic.

Check out this book's twin as well: *Creative Problem-Solving in Ethics* (Oxford University Press, 2007). Most of the methods and themes are similar, but you will find there a range of very different examples, differently developed. Creativity is so vital in ethics, and so underrated there, that it needs a book of its own.

SOURCES

Chapter 1: "At the Bus Stop" came to my father via e-mail. I regret not being able to give further attribution. The story of the buried rock I found first in Bill Mollison, *Permaculture* (Tagari, 1988), a book that is itself a beautiful extended example of creative thinking applied to environmental issues.

Chapter 2: Something like the random-word method appears in nearly every creativity text, including those cited above. I have expanded it to include other kinds of exotic association. On morphine, see Ronald Melzack, "The Tragedy of Needless Pain," *Scientific American* 262:2 (1990).

Chapter 3: The methods developed here also come from a variety of sources, and some of them are discussed in more detail in the Levine and de Bono books cited above. On the origins of brainstorming, see Alex Osborne's *Applied Imagination: Principles and Procedures of Creative Problem-Solving* (Creative Education Foundation, 1993).

Chapter 4: The two extended ideas with which this chapter ends can also be found on the Global Ideas Bank website (www.globalideasbank.org): check out "Couples for Community" by Ashlee Finecey and "Couples Choose New Middle Name" by me. I also published the naming idea many years ago in *Co-Evolution Quarterly* 41, (1984) and have heard from a number of couples who used it. The last exercise draws on Nalebuff and Ayres's book, cited above.

Chapter 5: The short quotation about TV in a child's room comes from Jane Brody, "TV's Toll on Young Minds and Bodies," *New York Times*, 8/3/04, p. D7. On viewing wastes as resources, see Paul Hawkins and Amory and Hunter Lovins, *Natural Capitalism* (Little, Brown, 1999). For the design of the recent Mars missions, see the official mission website (http://marsrovers.jpl.nasa.gov/gallery/video/animation.html).

Chapter 6: In addition to the Hawkins and Lovins book just cited, two other current books of radical change ideas are Bruce Mau and Jennifer Leonard, *Massive Change* (Phaidon, 2004), and David Bornstein, *How to Change the World: Social Entrepreneurs and the Power of New Ideas* (Oxford University Press, 2004). Frederick Turner's vision of living space vessels is drawn from his masterful and suggestive epic poem, *Genesis* (Dallas: Saybrook Publishing, 1988).

NOTES FOR TEACHERS

This book is intended primarily as a supplementary text for a university- or secondary-level critical thinking course, though it invites self-study as well, and should have applications in free-standing creativity courses too. On the critical thinking side, it is certainly not meant to cover the whole field: indeed, many vital analytical and argumentative skills are not even mentioned here. The job of this book is simply to add an equally vital dimension almost always overlooked. As I say in the preface, to be able to see the world in the light of possibility is a vital thinking skill as well. I believe it is one of the most vital of all.

The book is also intended to be self-explanatory. In class, head straight into *practice*. Each chapter's "For Practice" section gives you a good start. Students enjoy this kind of work; it gives concrete results that can make a real difference; and anyway, in the end, there is just no other way to develop the skills. Learning to think creatively is much more like learning to play piano, say, than learning music theory. Reading or lecturing about it can only be prelude.

Use the warm-ups and the wilder exercises, too. Even though they are less immediately practical, they help limber up the mind for the more serious work ahead and can introduce a note of playfulness that we sorely need as well.

Teachers unfamiliar with this material should take just a bit of care with their own initial attitudes. Creative thinking is not so familiar and can readily be undercut from our side as well: by not giving the methods enough time to work (especially the more improbable ones, like exotic association), by moving too fast to "edit" or tone down students' initial ideas once they do come up with them, or by hanging onto traditional formulations of problems (yes, well, let's just make cars a bit safer and more efficient. . . .). Teaching this material works best when teachers can whole-heartedly *model* the very attitudes that they are trying to teach. Give students a lot of space and a lot of provocation (for they too sometimes need to be nudged into *really using* some of these methods). And don't let them stop with ideas that are only a little out of the box. Look at their ideas midstream, but then challenge them to take their ideas to another level of creativity. Put students in brainstorming groups, or remix the groups if they're already working together. The sky is the limit here. Err on the side of asking too much, not expecting too little.

Students should be assigned to read through all of the "For Practice" sections, even if you do not require all of them for actual practice. There are substantive ideas and useful suggestions in those sections in any case, and students get a good sense of the range of problems they might tackle on their own.

The "For Practice" section of Chapter 6 ends the book by challenging students to take their results back out into the world and change some things. This is not so easy or so familiar either, but it can also be transformative not just of the world (we hope) but of individual students and indeed of the class as a whole. Consider closing the class, or this portion of it, with some such project. I would be honored to hear of these, as well as any other suggestions you might have for improving this book.